The New Blood Covenant In Christ

A Legal Redemptive Transaction!

All scripture is used from the King James Version of the Bible or is as indicated in the text.

All Greek and Hebrew definitions taken from "Strong's Exhaustive Concordance."

The New Blood Covenant In Christ
A Legal Redemptive Transaction!
ISBN 978-0-9766482-0-8

Cover art: Copyright © 1997 by Mark A. Lefler
Copyright © 2018 by Mark A. Lefler

Contact information for conference/speaking engagements:
Mark A. Lefler
126 Lake St
Yankton SD 57078
605-660-2742
throughtheveil7@gmail.com

Printed in the USA. All rights reserved under International Copyright law. Content and cover illustration may not be reproduced in whole or part in any form with or without the expressed written consdent of the copyright holder.

Published by Prairie Hearth Publishing, LLC
2310 Willowdale Rd
Yankton SD 57078

Luke 22:20

He also took the cup
after supper saying,
"This cup is the
New Covenant
in my blood, which
is shed for you."

Acknowledgements

Special thanks to close friends and Pastor J. Ratcliff for deep spiritual discussions on theological topics contained in this work.

"While traveling with Mark in Eastern Europe, I saw his incredible passion for souls and establishing the church on a solid foundation. Understanding the 'blood covenant' is the most important truth. Enjoy and learn." - Pastor John Ratcliff

Appreciation to Dr. B. J. Hunter for prayer and encouragment during development of this manuscript.

Foreword

The purpose of this book is to assist you in grasping some new Biblical concepts regarding your covenant in Christ. While this is not an exhaustive account, my intentions are to challenge preconceived religious ideas that have limited our ability to experience the fullness of God's love, and the benefits we should be partaking of as legally adopted children of God.

I hope to bring a fresh awareness to the circumstance fallen man is in, and the extravagant price that was paid in full for his acquittal. What is the price? Why, it was more than enough. And what are the continuing beneficial privileges the redeemed in Christ should be enjoying?

We'll explore the original objectives of blood covenant and put emphasis on faith in the blood of Jesus, who alone is our propitiation or mercy seat. His blood being the agent that ratified the Father's will to bring peace on earth, good will to men.

Hopefully you'll walk away from these truths with a new burning passion in your heart, with renewed confidence and boldness in approaching God through Christ. During life's journeys we all need to have an Emmaus encounter with Jesus that sets our heart ablaze with our first love.

CONTENTS

1. What is a Covenant 1
2. Dr. Livingstone and Henry Stanley 5
3. Stanley's Experience 9
4. Biology Review 13
5. Cutting a Blood Covenant 15
6. The Life Is In the Blood 19
7. Mankind, a Three-part Being 25
8. How Does this Relate? 31
9. You are Known 35
10. Activities of the Preincarnate Christ 43
11. Man's Condition 55
12. Birth Announcement 61
13. The Incarnation 63
14. A Better Way 67
15. Jesus' Blood Type 71
16. The Work of Redemption 74
17. The Veil of the Most Holy Place 85
18. First Fruit from the Grave 89
19. The Accession of Redemption 99
20. The Reveal 111
21. Where's That Coupon? 119
22. Benefits of the Blood 123
23. Jesus' Blood: A Weapon 132
24. Healing Through the Blood 151

CONTENTS

25. A New Identification 157
26. The Continuing Covenant Meal 159
27. Conclusion 165

CHAPTER 1
What Is A Covenant?

There are an array of applications for establishing a covenant. In more modern times, these needs have progressed to cover different and more complex agreements, but the primary reasons still revolve around three major topics. Business, protection and peace, and marriage and love are the main reasons for a covenant.

We rarely ever hear of a blood covenant in the U.S. other than native American blood brother agreements while watching an old western movie. This book's main focus will be concerned with historic blood covenant ceremonies from a Biblical perspective, and a comparison with carnal or worldly ceremonies, while discussing Christ's work of redemption.

Webster's dictionary defines covenant as: an agreement, a binding and solemn agreement made by two or more individuals, or parties. In business, there is normally the position that has the most to lose if the promises are not kept. Generally the money man. This party has the power to set most of the rules.

In protection it's normally the stronger party, be it a village or nation, that will protect the weaker or bring peace between adversaries. The NATO treaty is an example. Germany was our enemy and now an ally.

Marriage has promises and vows for life. I might add, if the bride is a virgin, blood is shed when the hymen membrane is broken during marital consummation. A sign of blood covenant.

The Hebrew word for covenant is agreement, from a verb signifying "to cut or divide," referring to a sacrificial custom in connection with covenant-making.

The seriousness of disgracing this type of agreement is not a fine, broken relationship, or incarceration, but payment was your life for being a covenant breaker. The lives of your whole family were at stake, and even they would hunt you down and kill you or turn you over to the avenger. To violate a sacred vow and its laws of agreement were such-a dishonor that a whole village could be annihilated as a result.

CHAPTER 2

Dr. Livingstone and Henry Stanley

To write a book featuring the topic of blood covenant, it's imperative that we hold a discussion on the experiences of two notable men of God that opened central Africa to the Gospel.

Dr. David Livingstone was a Scotsman who ascended from a poor family in Blantyre. He studied at and graduated from the University of Glasgow with degrees in theology and medicine. Livingstone would prove to become an accomplished explorer.

He must not have been an elegant expositor because the Missionary Society of London was hesitant to back him. The doors to China were closed and God opened one to Africa in 1841. Livingstone's calling pointed to the interior of Africa, and as he explored he introduced the inhabitants to Christianity.

Livingstone suffered many trials during his life of service. A lion attack severely injured his left arm, leaving it inoperative. Add to this malady the death of his wife due to malaria. Then, in 1865, on another expedition to locate the headwaters of the Nile, he was abandoned by his crew, who returned to Europe, declaring Livingstone's death.

Henry Stanley, a writer for the New York Herald, was dispatched to find Livingstone. A known atheist, Stanley would record his search in articles written for the newspaper. It was eight months before Stanley located Livingstone. His famous line, "Dr. Livingstone, I presume," is still remembered today.

During Stanley's time with Dr. Livingstone, he converted to Christianity, due to Livingstone's godly life, embodying the fruit of the Holy Spirit.

Stanley resupplied Livingstone, who had become deathly ill and returned to America.

In the next chapter, we'll discuss Stanley's experience with cutting a carnal blood covenant with a tribal king, which stopped the theft of his trade goods and supplies and gained his protection throughout the region from all possible dangerous African tribes as he searched for Dr. Livingstone.

CHAPTER 3

Stanley's Experience

When Stanley arrived in Africa, he surely went through some cultural shock, not having experienced tribal customs. During his eight-month search for Livingstone, he had many encounters with the native tribes. We will look at one of the most written and discussed encounters Stanley had with a powerful tribe chieftain that was well known in central Africa. This tribe was a very strong, fierce, warring nation, and their reputation preceded them.

Stanley was traveling with guides and an African interpreter as well as his safari accompaniment. He had entered Africa with a large quantity of supplies and trade goods. The necessary trade merchandise and provisions were imperative for survival and a successful search for Livingstone. These provisions were continually being stolen and to complicate the situation this war lord chieftain wanted Stanley's party under no certain terms to vacate his lands, and not ever return. Stanley didn't have the ability to fight off such a powerful tribal nation. Things looked bleak for the searchers until his young native interpreter confronted Stanley with the idea of cutting a strong covenant with the chief. When the ceremony was explained to him he found it to be repulsive and barbaric, however, as the situation continued to deteriorate, he reluctantly agreed with his African entrepreneur. The saving of the expedition was the benefit. He was told that everything this chieftain possessed would be at Stanley's disposal if he may need it. All through cutting a covenant.

After a few days of negotiations dealing with motives, and ability to keep agreements, they exchanged gifts. The chief wanted Stanley's white goat. His mind was made up on the issue. Stanley had been having serious stomach problems, and only the goat's milk would calm his ulcer down, and at times it was the only nourishment he had. Stanley finally released the goat to the chieftain. Stanley in return received the seven-foot copper wrapped spear of the chief. He felt he had gotten the short end of the gift trade.

The next step was the ritual, and it was interesting because both of the participants had proxies stand in to represent them, a young black man from the tribe and an English man for Stanley. The priest or holy man that I presume was from the tribe cut the wrists and let the blood of the two men drip into a cup of wine. The wine was then stirred, so the blood was thoroughly mixed. Then both men who received the incisions drank the wine. First, the English man and then the native man until all the wine was consumed.

At this point, the priest pronounced the blessings and curses that would fall on Stanley if he broke the covenant. Then his interpreter pronounced the curses on the chief, his wife, children, and tribe if he broke covenant with Stanley.

As a last step, they rubbed gun powder in the incisions to make the scars more noticeable in public so all would be reminded of the blood covenant between these brothers. Then trees that had a long life span were planted as a memorial to the covenant, and the king encouraged everyone to buy and trade with Stanley.

Stanley no longer needed to guard his trade goods for no one would steal from him, a blood brother. The penalty was death if they did, and that seven-foot spear he received proved to protect him and his party wherever they traveled. He was respected by the native tribes, and feared, for they were aware that the king chieftain and his warriors were behind Stanley. No one stole or hindered him after the blood covenant was ratified.

CHAPTER 4

Biology Review

I thought a brief review regarding our blood would be appropriate now. Let's focus our microscope and refresh our memory from high school biology class. First of all, what's blood made of, and what's its function in the human body?

Blood is a liquid and a solid. The liquid part is called plasma and is made of water, salts, and proteins. Fifty-five percent of our blood is plasma. The solids in our blood are made up of red and white blood cells with the remainder platelets accounting for 45% of human blood.

Red blood cells transport oxygen and nutrients to the lungs, tissues, and organs. They also carry waste, carbon dioxide to the lungs for exhalation and waste to the kidneys and liver, which filter and clean the blood.

White blood cells fight infection and are a part of the immune system.

Plasma's main function is to transport the blood cells throughout the body, along with nutrients and waste products.

Platelets help blood clot when you have a cut or wound, stopping bleeding and beginning the healing process.

There are four types of blood: A, B, AB, and O. Blood is either Rh-positive or Rh-negative. The Rh factor is important if you lose too much blood and need a transfusion.

So the Bible says life is in the blood, and when you're not feeling well, it's the first test given to discover what's going on inside you.

For example, if your platelets aren't functioning correctly, you can bleed to death or infection could take your life. Infected blood or not enough blood creates a threat to your physical existence.

CHAPTER 5

Cutting A Blood Covenant

The first step in cutting the blood covenant was to negotiate the terms and determine if each party could meet the demands.

The second was to cut oneself. Typically it was the arm or wrist. Blood was shed and mingled together. There were many approaches to accomplish this task.

The covenanters or spiritual leader presiding would mix the blood with wine, goats milk, or another beverage, and participants would drink all the content. They would press their wounds together and let the blood flow mix. This would seal them as one flesh.

They might also cut an animal in half, laying it divided on the ground and walk between the cut sides of meat in a figure-eight motion.

Listed below are a number of traditions that were practiced.

1) The participants would take on part of the others name.

2) The wounds from cuttings were dyed with pigment to make the scars more pronounced, so everyone would know that if you caused them trouble, you had to deal also with their blood covenant brother.

3) Monuments were set up, trees planted, flocks of their animals were interbred.

4) There was a covenant meal celebration. Each person involved would take a piece of bread and feed it to the other as a sign that all that I am is coming into you, and all you are is coming into me. Then, to end the ritual, a toast of wine was drunk.

5) Gifts were exchanged.

The benefits of a blood covenant always outweighed the penalty of breaking the vow. Stanley never knew of a covenant of this nature to have ever been broken in Africa, no matter the circumstances. Because of the repercussion, no one took advantage of his blood brother. It was unheard of. The blood covenant could not be annulled and generally would be respected into the next generations. Vile enemies, after cutting covenant, were loyal friends and brothers. Complete reconciliation was achieved as well as protection, financial, and physical needs. Blood brothers had one another's back. Just a thought to ponder: God goes before us, and He is our rear guard!

To conclude the blood covenant, blessings and curses were pronounced on both parties. All the wealth and power of each person was disclosed to the other. If ever a need emerged that demanded covenant help, your blood brother was there. This was the blessings of the agreement.

If one should break the blood covenant, the curses announced would fall on them. Which means basically your life was on the line.

CHAPTER 6

The Life Is In The Blood

As God begins to reveal Himself in Genesis we see Him establish a principle that will shape the future society of the Father's of Faith, that will carry on from Noah to the forming of the Nation of Israel till today. God instructs Noah in Genesis 9:4, "But you shall not eat flesh with its life, that is, its blood."

Moses instructs the Israelite to roast the Passover sacrifice of the Lord, and eat it. God is cultivating a respect for the blood of the animals that are killed and is applied to the lintel and doorpost of each house to protect the firstborn from the death angel. God would see the blood and pass over each house.

This is very significant because it begins to develop the role of the blood, cutting blood covenant, the blood of Christ and its application for our redemption, justification, and sanctification. Hebrews 9:14

So while carnal covenants drank and mingled blood, God forbid this behavior, for the life is in the blood, and it was the agent that covered the Jews' sin during the Old Testament covenant.

Leviticus 17:10 describes how serious God is about this topic, "And whatever man of the house of Israel, or of the strangers who dwell amongst them, who eats any blood, I will set my face against that person who eats blood, and will cut him off from among his people. For the life of the flesh is in the blood, and I have given it to you upon the altar to make atonement for your souls; for it is the blood that makes atonement for the soul (human life)." The blood is much too sacred to be misused or trivialized by eating or drinking it.

The Romans accused the early day Christians of cannibalism, "Saying we ate flesh and drank blood." This was a complete falsehood in not discerning Christ's body and blood. In John 6, Jesus feeds 5,000 and has dissertation on the following day in Capernaum, about the Bread of Life. Quite a quarrel erupted in their ranks and Jesus in verses 53 to 59 told the crowd, saying, "Most assuredly, I say to you, unless you eat the flesh of the Son of Man and drink His blood you have no life in you." Jesus expounded on this through verse 59. Obviously, they didn't discern the supernatural implications of this, and the disciples choked on these hard sayings and departed.

This theme of respecting blood continues on into the New Testament covenant after the death, burial, and resurrection of Jesus. At the first meeting, Paul and Barnabas had with the Jerusalem Council, a discussion broke out concerning Gentile believers' adherence to old Jewish laws and the customs of Moses. This account is found in Acts chapter 15. The conclusion was basically this: the law was insufficient in changing the fallen, evil condition of the heart of man, and not until salvation by faith were Jewish believers purified. Gentile believers were cleansed without the law and circumcision, being filled with the Holy Spirit. Verses 28 and 29 sum up the only restrictions to be maintained for Gentile converts.

Acts 15:24-29

"For it seemed good to the Holy Spirit, and to us, to lay upon you no greater burden than these necessary things: that you abstain from things offered to idols, from blood, from things strangled, and from sexual immorality. If you keep yourselves from these, you will do well."

This is a pretty straightforward directive. It's no mystery when we see no power in most fellowships today, for we traded the power of God for new religious traditions that unfortunately make God's word of no effect, just like the Pharisees and Sadducees (Mark 7:8-13).

Some churches tend to go to the extremes of performance and doctrine as Ephesus did in Revelation 2, forgetting the weightier matters of love and mercy, while others gravitate toward no accountability at all and lose their candlestick!

These pendulum swings are probably a result of believers putting their faith in the wisdom of men and not in the power of God, which was the passionate driving force of the apostle, Paul.

I Corinthians 2:1-5

Vs 2 "And my speech and my preaching was not with the enticing words of man's wisdom, but in demonstration of the Spirit and of power;"

Vs 3 "That your faith should not stand in the wisdom of men, but in the power of God."

It is vital for us to understand how we were created to grasp the significance of mankind's fall. It is essential so we can comprehend the role of Christ's blood in our redemption.

CHAPTER 7

Mankind: A Three Part Being

To understand the Biblical account of the Incarnation, we need to understand how God created us. We are told in Genesis we are created in His image, according to God's likeness, Genesis 1:26. It is clear at this time God did not have a human body. We will cover this later in another chapter.

The New Testament scriptures reveal we are a three-part being.

I Thessalonians 5:23, King James Version, announces our makeup, "And the very God of peace sanctify you wholly; and I pray God your whole spirit, soul and body be kept blameless unto the coming of our Lord Jesus Christ."

Moffat Translation: "May the God of Peace consecrate you through and through! Spirit, soul, and body, may you be kept without break or blame till the arrival of our Lord Jesus;" vs 24, "He who calls you is faithful, he will do this."

Let's look closer at these three parts and see how Hebrew and Greek definitions bring clarity and separation.

SPIRIT

The word "spirit" in Greek is "pneuma" (#4151), "meaning current of air, breath or breeze, spirit, which, like the wind, is invisible, immaterial and powerful, superhuman, an angel, demon or divine, Holy Spirit, Christ." Our spirit is the most integral part of our human make up because it is the eternal aspect of our existence. When our body stops functioning, our spirit departs. It's that old adage, "He gave up the ghost." God is a spirit and those that worship Him must worship Him in Spirit and in Truth!

We can conclude that when God breathed into Adam (which means "red clay") the breath of life, Adam, became a living soul. Genesis 2:7

Soul here in Hebrew means a breathing creature. Nephesh (#5315) is used very widely, encompassing breathing creatures, the whole life itself that includes the soulish spirit. In context, we, in a general sense, can say Adam received his spirit and soul and fleshly body life actively energized (zoe, "life as God has it"). When God breathed a current of life-creating power into the nostrils of his hollow, lifeless shell.

SOUL

The second integral part of our human make up is the soul that 1 Thessalonians 5:23 describes. The Greek word for soul used here is "psyche" (#5590), denoting "the breath of life, and the soul in its various meanings." Here is a list of those attributes: the natural life of the body, the seat of personality, own self, seat of the essence of man by which he perceives, reflects, feels, desires, will and purpose, seat of appetite and desire.

The text we are using has already listed spirit apart from soul, and I assure you the Holy Spirit was not confused on this issue when he inspired the writing of this verse. I am thoroughly convinced that the use of soul here is our emotional, reasoning personality.

Hebrews Chapter 4:12, Moffat Translation:

"For the Logos of God is a living thing, active and more cutting than any sword with double edge, penetrating to the very division of soul and spirit, joints and marrow, scrutinizing the very thoughts and conceptions of the heart."

The language here suggests extreme difficulty distinguishing between our soul and spirit, but we are to deny the flesh and walk in our new spirit, that's regenerated, quickened, born again so we will not fulfill the lust of the soulish flesh. Galatians 5:16

So, relatively speaking, the spirit is the higher and stronger over the soul, the lower component. They are separate, but intertwined, revealing how important it is for us to renew our minds to agree with God and His kingdom. For sure, the word and the Holy Ghost can determine the two, and will help us on our way to walk in the fruit of the Spirit and deny our flesh.

Remember, God is working in you both to will and to do His good pleasure. He will accomplish it. We need to abide in the vine and agree with Him. He has a good future and hope for you.

BODY

The third part of our personal composition is our earthly body. Before Adam's treason in the Garden of Eden, there was no death, sickness or diseases to abate the natural body. However, now our spirit is sewn into a corruptible body, in dishonor, in weakness (I Corinthians 15:42-44). We have all experienced a funeral at one time or another, and probably won't miss our own. "Rapture quick, now please!" The Greek word for body is "soma" (#4983), "the body as whole, the instrument of life." I would say it is the container that houses your spirit and soul, that allows you to touch, feel, experience physical life in the terrestrial world. This affords us the opportunity to know and build a loving relationship with God through Christ's atonement for Adam's catastrophic disaster, which befell the human race. Let's continue.

The "body" is not the man, for he himself can't exist apart from his body. As stated previously, your spirit and soul carry on for eternity. For those in Christ, their corruptible will put on incorruption, this mortal must put on immortality (vs 53). Verse 49 tells us flesh and blood cannot inherit the kingdom of God, but we will be changed and have a new body like unto Jesus.

So, in conclusion, we can say of ourselves, "we are a spirit (pneuma) that lives forever. We have a soul (psyche), our mind, will, and emotions. We live in a body (soma) that allows us to live in, move, and have being in the mortal realm."

CHAPTER 8

How Does This Relate?

Now that we have established that you were created spirit, soul, and body, let's look at when your spirit was created to help us see Jesus in a later chapter in his pre-existing spiritual form before His incarnation. We will evaluate how these truths relate to who we are, our legal redemption in Christ, that justifies us before God.

The first hurdle, which isn't a leap of faith, God needed physical blood to allow Him to cut covenant with fallen man. If you recall, animals were secured by Abram in proxy for God when He cut covenant. Abram's name changed to Abraham, meaning father of a multitude. That's a lot of stars. Circumcision was started as a sign of covenant, and blood was shed on the human side of the agreement. We'll make a comparison of the Abrahamic and The New Covenant in a later chapter.

Most Christians are familiar with the following scriptures that are associated with the unborn.

Jeremiah 1:5 "Before I formed you in the belly, I knew you, and before you came forth out of the womb I sanctified (set apart) you, I ordained you a prophet unto the nations."

Ps. 139:14 "We are fearfully and wonderfully made."

We can plainly see in the first line of this verse that God knew Jeremiah before he was a fetus in his mother's womb. It appears God knew him by his spirit. Zechariah tells us God formed the spirit of man within him.

Zechariah 12:1 "The burden of the word of the Lord for Israel; saith the Lord, which stretched forth the Heavens, and layeth the foundations of the Earth, and formeth the spirit of man within him."

Isaiah 42:5 "Thus says God the Lord, Who creates the Heavens and stretches them out, Who spreads out the Earth and that which comes from it, Who gives breath to those that walk on it: And spirit to those who walk on it."

God gives breath to everything that's alive. However, we are made in His image and likeness and have an eternal spirit. God gives us our breath and spirit. Again we see God forms the spirit of man, and it is the candle of the Lord (Proverbs 20:27).

Last scripture and most obvious is Ecclesiastes 12:7. This chapter deals with the passing of man. "Then the dust will return to the earth as it was, and the spirit will return to God who gave it."

So the truth in these passages tell us the following; God knew us before we were in the womb, He formed our spirit. When we die, our spirit returns to Him who gave it, and our spirit is the candle of the Lord.

"For all things were created through Him and for Him." (Colossians 1:16)

In conclusion, our parents created our embryo, but God Himself created our spirit that will live forever. Eternity began for each of us when our life began in our mother's womb.

CHAPTER 9

You Are Known

We have settled that God knew us in the womb and before the womb. These truths can create a new hurdle on some popular theology. Our Heavenly Father is involved in every conception creating the eternal spirit of each human being. From fingerprints, to DNA, to your eye scan, you are distinctly original. That's probably why God is not willing that any should perish, but all come to repentance (2 Peter 2: 9).

Romans 11 :29 further tells us that the gifts and calling of God are irrevocable. While this quote is in regards to Israel it pertains to the overall gospel message. The Greek word for calling is "Klesis" (2821). It actually means invitation, and gifts charisma (5486) means a gift of grace, God as the donor of His free bestowment upon sinners.

Salvation and all that accompanies it, deliverance, from danger, as well as spiritual endowments, are given. It appears that God foreknew, foreknows, and foreordained you, (Greek word proginosko, 4267, which means to know beforehand), before you by an act of your will chose to receive His gift of grace, salvation through faith in Jesus. The gift of salvation and the invitation to respond are extended to all of humanity and will not be reversed by God. Just as Adam in the garden had a free choice, so does the rest of mankind. Adam didn't choose wisely.

IT'S YOUR CHOICE

Jesus, on the last day of the Feast of Tabernacles, stood up and cried out," If anyone thirsts, let him come to Me and drink. He who believes in me, as the scripture has said, out of his heart will flow rivers of living water (John 7:37, 38).

After Jesus's death, burial, and resurrection in Revelation 22:17, the same invitation is given that includes the Church representing the Kingdom of God on Earth, the spirit and the bride say, "'Come! And let him who hears say, 'Come!' And let him who thirsts come. Whoever desires let him take the water of life freely." There is always more room for more of God's love, which is shed abroad in our hearts by the Holy Spirit.

When Jesus on the cross said it is finished, the suffering for sin, he bowed His head and gave up the ghost. The veil in the Temple separating the Holy of Holies from the outer courts was torn from top to bottom, and exposed the Ark of the Covenant.

Only the high priest had access once a year to enter during Passover to sprinkle blood on the mercy seat for a covering to protect the Israelites from the judgement of their sins that year.

It was also called the day of atonement. It is imperative that we understand and grasp the significance of this event because everything changed. The law limited access given in the Old Covenant. A new and living way was now available through Jesus. No more killing of animals for blood atonement for sin, but an open door policy to come boldly to the throne of grace that we may obtain mercy and find grace to help in time of need. We have a great risen High Priest that has passed through the Heavens, and now ever liveth to make intercession on our behalf with God. Everyone is welcome to enter through the open door. John 10:9. "Jesus said, 'I am the door, if anyone enters by me, he will be saved, and will go in and out and find pasture.'" This 24/7 open access to fellowship with our Heavenly Father, who I might add adopted us into his family, is secured by Jesus' blood that speaks from the mercy seat in Heaven better things than the blood of Abel. Abel's blood, after Cain murdered him, cried out for vengeance. Christ's blood speaks out, "Forgive them, Father, they know not what they do," deliverance and wholeness, soundness, and healing (Hebrews 12: 22-24). This is not a universal proclamation that everyone is pardoned, but the declaration that the provision of mercy through sacrifice is complete. It bestows the invitation to come to the Master's table and dine at the Covenant feast to behold the beauty of the Lord and embrace His Agape Love. An invitation of restoration from Adams failure, as if we wouldn't have succumbed to the same fate. We've all sinned and come up short of perfection. Get in and stay in the palm of God's hand. When everyone else has seemed to forsake you, He'll be your Father, Mother, spouse and best friend. He has your name inscribed in the palm of His hand. His blood is speaking out to you and over you of His enduring love. Not based on your performance but on Jesus' performance. Behold the perfect lamb of God, slain from the foundation of the world. Your failures haven't surprised Him. He already had accurately diagnosed your issue and orchestrated the cure that would satisfy His righteous judgment for your sin.

FREE WILL

God gives the invitation, the call to receive the gift of salvation, to every person's spirit He has foreknown and created. And those who change their mind (repent), and believe with child-like faith, are justified before the court in Heaven, their trespasses being forgiven, having the ordinances of broken law and requirements wiped out that held a guilty verdict over , and walk in the spirit as Christ did. He is now in us, so where you go He goes, so we should start getting better results in our life. As He is, so are we in this world (1 John 1:17).

Look at 2 Corinthians 4: 6 and 7. It tells us God shined His light into our hearts, putting His glorious treasure in earthen vessels that the excellence of the power may be of God and not us. Verses 10 and 11 show us that, even during hard times, our Father's will is to manifest the life of Jesus in our mortal body. We can reign in life through the one, Jesus Christ, who has given us abundant grace and the gift of righteousness (Romans 5:17).

To those who have been called, born again, justified, and are being conformed like Christ, will be glorified receiving a new body like Jesus's resurrected body when their spirit vacates the old one at death. This has been a breakdown of Romans 8 vs. 29 and 30 to give a perspective that humanity will be accountable before the divine jurisprudence of God by willingly neglecting so great a salvation. God is not electing who responds, but knows who will and who won't. Like sowing and reaping, God sowed His Son into the earth and knows there will be a harvest of souls throughout every generation. As I stated earlier, God is not willing that any should perish but that all would come to repentance. He takes no joy in judging the wicked. They were created to have relationship with Him. Look at Deuteronomy 30: 19:

"I call Heaven and earth as witnesses today against you, that I have set before you life and death, blessing and cursing; therefore choose life, that both you and your descendants may live."

God is really saying here, "Don't be stiff-necked and hard-hearted. Take life and its blessings."

You are a free-will agent concerning all the Covenant Promises of God.

CHAPTER 10

Activities Of The Preincarnate Christ

Well, now that we've taken a look at how we're created, let's investigate how and why God sent his son, and what Jesus was doing before receiving a mortal body to inhabit.

In Revelation 13:8, the second half of the verse, (b) "lamb slain from the foundation of the world." The lamb here being Jesus and the plan of redemption was already in play before the creation. So God wasn't nervous when Adam fell prey to Satan's schemes. His strategy, Jesus, was already our provision.

David said, "I saw my Lord say to my Lord, 'Sit thou at my right hand till all your enemies are put under your feet.'" (Psalm 110:1) Jesus was present with God the Father in Heaven, a supernatural being. A little research into the old covenant will astonish you just how busy Jesus was in the spiritual plans of our Heavenly Father's Kingdom.

W. E. Vine's "Expository Dictionary of Biblical Words," shines a halogen light beam on Christ's activities under the title of "The Angel of the Lord." There are three categories that appear. The Hebrew word for angel is malakh (#4397) messenger angel.

A. First, there are the prophetic messengers, "men sent by God to deliver His message because of His compassion for His people; but they mocked the messengers of God, despised His Word, and misled His prophets, until the wrath of God arose against His people, till there was no remedy." (2nd Chronicles, 36:15-16)

2nd Corinthians 11:3 Corrupted from the simplicity that is in Christ.

B. There were also angelic messengers. The English word angel is etymological, (the origin and development of words, tracing back as far as its own language, to its source) related to the Greek word angelos, whose translation is similar to the Hebrew "messenger or angel." The angel is a supernatural messenger of the Lord sent with a particular message. For example the two angels sent to Lot at Sodom (Genesis 19:1). These two angels were commissioned to protect Lot.

C. The third and most significant are the phrases "malak Yaweh, the angel of the Lord," and malak Elohim, "the angel of God."

This messenger we will examine closely. The above phrase is always used in the singular. It appears there is not more than one. It denotes an angel who had mainly a saving and protective function. Protection (Exodus 23:23). He may also bring about destruction, (1st Chronicles 21:16). Note the angel stands between the earth and the heavens.

The relationship between the Lord and the "angel of the Lord" is often so close it is difficult to separate the two. This identification has led some interpreters to conclude that the angel of the Lord was the pre-incarnate Christ.

Genesis 16:7 Then the angel of the Lord intervenes for Hagar and again for Ishmael.

Genesis 21:17 Due to the covenant in Genesis 17 with special attention to verses 10 and 11, "This is the covenant which you shall keep, between you and thy seed after; every man child among you shall be circumcised." This included, unfortunately, to Ishmael, the first child, not just the promised Isaac. The Angel of the Lord upheld the covenant.

Exodus 3:2 The angel of the Lord appears in the burning bush before Moses. "Take off your shoes from off your feet, for the place you stand is holy ground." He receives worship, verse 14 (NIV). The conversation the divine one speaking goes from the "Angel of the Lord" to God saying, "I AM that I AM." A sign of the Trinity, no separation between God and the messenger.

Judges 6:1 God sends a flesh prophet to warn his people; they disobey.

Judges 6:11 The "Angel of the Lord" then calls Gideon.

Genesis 22:11 Just before Abraham plunged the knife into Isaac as a sacrifice, the Angel of the Lord intervenes, and said, "Abraham, lay not thine hand upon the lad, neither do thou anything unto him . . ." and provides a ram in the thicket.

Daniel 2:15 Further accounts are Shadrack, Meshack, and Abednego in the fiery furnace and a fourth one in the fire "is like the Son of God."

Daniel 6:22, "My God has sent His Angel and shut the lions' mouths." While this account doesn't say the "Angel of the Lord," this setting again refers to singular, one particular angel. We are aware that God created all the angels, noting that one-third chose not to serve Him. The narrative points to the "Angel of the Lord" protecting His prophet Messenger. You weigh the evidence.

Genesis 31:11 Jacob is told by the "Angel of the Lord" to return to the land of his kindred. He then prays to the God of his fathers, to the Lord in chapter 32:9, (the angel of the Lord) who told him to return to his homeland. The result is a wrestling match with one whom he thinks is a man. The outcome is his realization it was God, whom he declares, "I have seen God face to face," and renames the location Peniel, gets a new name (Israel), and limps away to encounter his brother whom he's supplanted – Esau.

No man has seen the face of God and lived, Exodus 33:30. So who did Jacob wrestle with that was God? The pre-incarnate Christ.

We again see this intrinsic union between the Angel of the Lord and God working in harmony to accomplish their goal, the birth of a nation.

Joshua 5:13-15 Joshua was near Jericho and lifts up his eyes and behold a man stood opposite him and said, "Are you for us or for our adversaries?" (verse 14). "No but as Commander of the Army of the Lord I have now come." Joshua fell on his face and worshipped. This commander instructs Joshua to take off his sandals, "for the place where you stand is Holy."

Just as Jacob encountered a man, now Joshua has, too. The outcome of each is the realization it's a divine experience. Joshua worships, removing his shoes as did Moses at the burning bush, and Jacob sees God face to face, the Angel of the Lord.

Finally, in my last comparison (I realize this has been a bit laborious), I'm laying a foundation for a purpose, and that would be for your benefit. So let's investigate John's encounter and another one, Daniel experienced.

Revelation 22:8, 9 "Now I John saw and heard these things, and when I heard and saw, I fell down to worship before the feet of the angel who showed me these things. Then he said to me, 'See that you do not do that.' For I am your fellow servant and of your brethren the prophets, and of those who keep the word of this book, Worship God." We see the same reaction in Revelation 19:10. That this messenger angel likewise will not receive worship.

So it is clear the regular messenger angels will not receive worship that belongs to God alone. Any form of idolatry must never be allowed.

John does fall at the feet of Jesus in the vision recorded in Revelation 1:17, a sign of worship and humility.

Daniel 10:10 Daniel is on his hands and knees trembling before an angel that has striking similarities in description to Jesus in Revelation 1:17. This supernatural messenger does accept a worshipful posture from Daniel. He does manage to stand trembling after being strengthened and told to stand. This is a very convincing comparison between these two supernatural messengers who both receive worship. The evidence points to this angel of the Lord, being the pre-incarnate Christ. This is noted in Matthew Henry's Commentary, Volume One, page 1100, Chapter 10 of Daniel.

III. A description of that glorious person whom Daniel saw in a vision, which, it is generally agreed, could be no other than Christ himself, the eternal Word.

Some would say how could the pre-incarnate spirit of Christ be withstood for three weeks by the demon controlling over the kingdom of Persia. Adam forfeited the authority to Satan that God had given him. Satan, the god of this world, the principalities of wickedness, spiritual darkness, rulers of this fallen world, took control.

Jesus has not come to earth yet in physical form to legally regain control, destroy death and retain the keys of hell and death (I John 3:8) "For this purpose was the Son of God manifested to destroy the works of the devil. Colossians 2:15: "And having spoiled principalities and powers, he made a show of them openly, triumphing over them in it." Therefore we can reason that God almighty recognized the illegitimately gained authority Satan held through wicked means.

Our Heavenly Father could find no one greater to swear by to Abraham, so He swore by Himself. He is just, His counsel is perfect, faultless. God is righteous in all His judgements, and there is no darkness and shadow of turning with Him. His own standard of holiness He meets 100%. So payment must meet His jurisdictional authority, for He has the legal power to decide. After all, He made everything!

Here's the point I'm making: God was patient and had to wait till His appointed time to send Jesus. Until then, due to Adam, death reigned and Satan had basically a free hand. It was permitted him authority due to the desire of Adam to know good and evil. God recognized this jurisdiction Satan had, because Adam gave it to him. Satan tried to tempt Jesus in the wilderness, Matthew 4:9, with all his fallen kingdom and Jesus refused. He had come to regain God's creation and meet God's righteous standard. Now mankind has a choice in whom he serves. While it may appear the world is out of control, God is not slack concerning his promises but is long suffering for all to come to repentance. When the church age ends and Christ comes out of the east mounted on his white charger, it will not be a loving experience for those on earth. He returns as the conquering King of Kings to rule and judge with a rod of iron.

In conclusion of this chapter, the primary thought I want to convey is that Jesus was and is first a supernatural being, "Angel of God," carrying out kingdom business before His incarnation to earth. Now we can, in the next chapter, discuss how did God end up inside Mary's womb, the first step toward our salvation and a new blood covenant.

You might be asking yourself why did Jesus have to come to earth, on numerous occasions he had already appeared as a man. God's spiritual messengers can appear as a physical man. God wrestles with Jacob, Joshua sees the commander of the armies of Heaven, Paul in Hebrews 13:2 tells us to not forget to entertain strangers, for by so doing some have entertained angels unaware. So why did our Heavenly Father send his son to take on human flesh? Human blood was needed to cut a new covenant and graft in the gentile nations, who were in past times without God, estranged aliens from the commonwealth of Israel, complete strangers from the covenants of Promise, having no hope and without God in the world (Ephesians 2:12).

What Adam had lost in the immortal realm had to be conquered and won back in the natural realm as well.

For further study, a comparison of the most high priest of God, King of Salem (Peace), who met Abraham and received alms, the King of Righteousness, who had no beginning or end of days, genealogy. Jesus, now our High Priest after the priesthood order of Melchizedek, a supernatural order and not after Aaron, who is carnal and of the law. Jesus, now as conqueror of the world, prevailed through the flesh, without sin, to rightfully fill the new order, a new priesthood, dispersing grace, mercy and truth through the new blood covenant. (Hebrews 7; Genesis 14:18)

54

CHAPTER 11

Man's Condition

Today a large percentage of ministries focus on convincing people how wicked a wretched sinner they are and going to the extremes of labeling different levels of severity of transgressions and God's judgments. A modern day inquisition. It is true that all have sinned and fallen short of the Glory, the presence of God. He is either with you or not. So if you miss it by an inch or a mile, your condition hasn't changed. We all got in this position because of Adam, so the focus isn't completely on you, but legal spiritual grounds imposed on us. His treason passed on to all mankind. Let's have a look at Romans 5:12:

"Therefore, just as through one man (Adam) sin entered the world, and death through sin, and so death spread to all men, because all have sinned."

Ezekiel 18:20

"The soul who sins shall die. The son shall not suffer for the iniquity of the father, nor the father for the iniquity of the son. The righteousness of the righteous shall be upon himself, and the wickedness of the wicked shall be upon himself."

Chapter 18:1-3 of Ezekiel declares that the parable about sons suffering for the iniquity of their fathers shall no longer be used in Israel, but that individuals will be responsible for their own sin. Remember, the Gentile nations were outside the Old Covenant promises and sacrificial system for removal of trespasses against God by breaking the given law.

An iniquity is an evil perversity, twisted, crooked fault, to do wickedly. Just flat out sin. This behavior can be learned and emulated by siblings within a family. When demonic activity is present, the outcome can plunge generations into a chain of continued types of sin. It can twist moral realities into thoughtless perversions which are not just sexual in nature.

That's a big thank you Adam, you aren't our hero! God then gave the law to try and restrain the moral depravity after He already washed away a population with a flood. When you're deficient at your core, the heart, no external restriction can continually hold back a nature prone to rebellion. Here enters the principality of the air, Satan, the god of this world, the rulers of the darkness of this age, spiritual hosts of wickedness in the heavenly places (Ephesians 6:12).

Satan comes in lying to tempt us and destroy and in the end kill us through continued separation from our Creator (John 10:10).

Sin can be so subtle it sneaks in unaware. A brief examination of James 2:9 reveals that God's not happy about partiality. Those that sin are convicted by the law. The root of partiality is really a form of self-righteousness and fear. The self-righteous esteems themselves better than the poor and seat them on the floor by their feet, and the rich who oppress them are elevated to a location of favor whom they fear. Evil thoughts of judgment prevail. Perfect love casts out fear and is only received by the humble. So whoever will keep the whole law and yet stumble in one point is guilty of all. There's no curve on the grading scale.

Love doesn't put down but lifts up. Love is the value scale.

Later in the same chapter in verses 9-13, James uses adultery and murder as examples of sin, and the conclusion is the same: a transgressor of the law. We can conclude the law is a tutor to prove to ourselves we don't have a passing grade. All our own religious efforts fail. This work mentality has failed to produce real fruit and created a performance-based lie that leads to self-righteousness, legalism and hypocrisy.

THE REST OF THE STORY

Here's the rest of the bad news. When you were born, and your Spirit was manifested in your body, you were not in relationship with God, your Creator. We all have been born under the law of Sin and Death that Adam released on all mankind, to know good and evil and the greatest deception of Satan, to be like God. This treason broke Adam and Eve's relationship with God and got them removed from the Garden of Eden before an attempt to partake from the Tree of Life.

Had the fallen gotten and eaten from the Tree of Life, they would have had eternal life and that fate would have kept them and us from ever having a possibility of personal relationship with our Creator. Satan could have destroyed God's plan of family, love and fellowship.

Tragic enough to now be in bondage to the Law of Sin and Death, but now add to it Exodus 20:5.

"For I the Lord your God am a jealous God, visiting the iniquity of the fathers upon the children to third and fourth generations of those who hate me."

This curse is ongoing right now, continually before our eyes. What a picture of a snowball effect, getting bigger and out of control. The work of redemption and becoming a new creation in Christ, Christ Jesus is the only way these curses are broken (Galatians 3:13, 14).

"Christ has redeemed us from the curse of the law, having become a curse for us (for it is written, 'Cursed is everyone who hangs on a tree') that the blessings of Abraham might come upon the Gentiles in Christ Jesus, that we might receive the promise of the Spirit through faith."

SELF INFLICTED

At the end of the day, our condition is being alienated from God. Mainly due to Adam's failure, not our own. However, we compound our predicament with our own personal sins and wound our spirit, emotions, and body, as well as others. Sin can be fun for a season, till you realize you've been bitten by a snake. Also people can become vulnerable to demonic activity and oppression. How else can you look around at this chaotic world and understand why it seems to be coming unglued? Right is wrong and wrong is right!

We should be grateful that we weren't left in these conditions. God in His perfect plan and timing sent the Promised One to rescue His creation from captivity. Not leaving us to our own devices.

CHAPTER 12
Birth Announcement

Even God sent out birth announcements for His son. First through angelic hosts to the common men, shepherds, on duty in the fields, protecting their herds at night.

Luke2: 8-14 (11) "For unto you is born this day in the city of David a savior which is Christ the Lord. (12) Glory to God in the highest and on Earth peace, good will toward men."

Secondly, through a just and devout man, Simeon, who was waiting for the Messiah. It was revealed by the Holy Spirit he would not see death before he saw the Lord's Christ. Simeon was led by the Holy Spirit to the temple. He was present when Jesus' parents arrived with him to keep the law of purification, a sacrifice for reconciliation for Mary and to present Jesus to the Lord. Simeon took up Jesus in his arms, saying in prayer, "Lord now let your servant depart in peace for my eyes have seen thy salvation which you have prepared before the face of all the people. A light to bring revelation to the Gentiles, and the glory of your people Israel."

Also the prophetess Anna was present and spoke of Jesus to all there who looked for redemption in Israel. We see all things being established by two or three witnesses.

CHAPTER 13
The Incarnation

Genesis 1:28 "God created man and woman and blessed them; Be fruitful and multiply, fill the Earth and subdue it."

The 8th chapter clarified that our parents did not create our eternal spirit, but only the natural body that contains it, which is significant. So our spirit is within us but at what point did this transpire? I believe that, at conception, life begins. God sends our created spirit to inhabit us. He formed our inward parts, and covered us in our mother's womb (Psalm 139: 13-17).

Verse 14, "I will praise thee, for I'm fearfully and wonderfully made: marvelous are thy works, and that my soul knoweth right well."

"Soul" in this verse is the Hebrew word "nephesh"

(5314), meaning to be breathed upon, becoming a breathing creature. Adam came alive when God breathed into his lifeless clay shell. God knew Jeremiah before he was even in his mother's belly. My question is, was this foreknowledge or was Jeremiah's spirit created in Heaven then sent to fill his fleshly body?

We don't know exactly the timing of Jeremiah's spirit being created, either at the time of his conception or a time frame in Heaven before he entered his earthly embryo.

At this juncture, I don't have enough scripture or illumination to prove one way or the other. The word in Hebrew for "know" or "knew" is YADA and is used in a broad variety of meanings : to know by observation, care, instruction, designation and so on goes the definitions. Our parents created our physical body. God created our spirit, the eternal part of us that lives forever.

We can rest assured that God knows every human with foreknowledge better than they know themselves.

However, we do know that Jesus was translated

from Heaven or the supernatural realm into Mary. Mary being a virgin, not having known a man physically, so this life was a supernatural physical creation. Jesus's spirit manifested into Mary's womb, and the Holy Ghost breathed life into Christ's embryo. This is the opposite of what happened for us. We had a tissue cell structure and no eternal spirit. So the timing of when we received our spirit isn't as important as when it was regenerated when we were born again of incorruptible seed by the word and Holy Spirit. There was only one limitation God had, and that was He needed Mary's consent to allow this pregnancy to happen.

Luke 1: 26-38 In verse 38 Mary said, "Behold the handmaid of the Lord; be it unto me according to your word, and the Angel Gabriel departed from her. So Mary agreed to have the Holy Ghost overshadow her. She was with child and the hymen membrane was not broken. Emanuel, God is now among us.

"In whom we have redemption through his blood, even the forgiveness of sins."
Colossians 1:14

CHAPTER 14

A Better Way

Hebrews 10:4 and 5: "For it is not possible that the blood of bulls and of goats should take away sins. Wherefore when he comes into the world, he said, Sacrifice and offering you did not want, but a body You have prepared for me.'"

This is a prophetic scripture from Psalms 40:6, real straight forward about Jesus. God the Father created a physical body for Jesus's spirit to dwell in.

Another scripture that reinforces this point is Hebrews 2:9.

"But we see Jesus, who was made a little lower than the angels for the suffering of death, crowned with glory and honor; that He by the grace of God, should taste death for every man."

Hebrews 2:14 "As the children are partakers of

flesh and blood, He also himself (Jesus) likewise took part of the same, flesh and blood that through death He might destroy him that had the power of death, that is the devil, and deliver them who through fear of death were all their lifetime subject to bondage."

Jesus became a man without sin to carry our guilty sentence and destroy Satan's dominion over us and set us free from death.

It wasn't God's plan, although He wasn't surprised. He didn't want the whole sacrificial system. It was forced into operation by Adam's sin to cover the rebellious nature man had acquired through his newfound knowledge of evil. God took no pleasure in these offerings because they were mandatory by law, not of love and true repentance toward relationship.

Hebrews 10:9 is a quote of Jesus speaking, "Lo I come to do thy will oh, God." He came to remove the first sacrificial system and replace it himself, offering His life and blood to redeem mankind. It's an offering motivated by compassion, mercy, and love. His blood was shed to cut a new Covenant with humanity. Jesus' scourging and crucifixion satisfied God's wrath on sin, and also displayed His good will to justify and forgive all who believe and receive the Lord Jesus Christ.

It's interesting to note that God didn't have blood to cut covenant with Abram. So animals were used temporarily till Christ would come. Abraham received circumcision as man's cutting and a sign of the old covenant.

The only begotten son of God could not be born under the curse that Adam passed on to everyone. That is the law of Sin and Death. So what makes Jesus' blood different from any one else?

Righteous. Positive.

CHAPTER 15
Jesus' Blood Type

I don't have a clue what type of blood Jesus had. What I do know is, it wasn't tainted by the sin of Adam or the law of Sin and Death that infected all human beings on earth. Jesus was in perfect relationship with his heavenly Father.

Secondly, there was no generational curse on Christ that flows down on the children of earthly fathers that hated God (Exodus 20:15).

2 Corinthians 5:21 tells us Jesus had never sinned against his Father.

Interlinear Greek-English New Testament literal translation: "For he made the (one) who knew no sin (to be) sin on our behalf, that we might become (the) righteousness of God in Him."

Weymouth translation: "He made him who knew

nothing of sin to be sin for us, in order that we in Him may become the righteousness of God."

Jesus became our violation before God his Father. He was perfect in all of his ways and without spot or blemish. I like to describe the blood of Jesus in this perspective: His blood type was God's in an undefiled human form, righteous, positive. Though our sins be scarlet, they can be cleansed white as snow by the blood of Christ.

When the revelation of
your redemption
reflects the measure of
Christ's suffering
you'll no longer want to
offend love with your liberty!

CHAPTER 16

The Work Of Redemption

In an earlier chapter we discussed the Jewish Nation and how God had cultivated a respect for blood with them, because life is in the blood and it was given to cover the sins committed by His people as an atonement on the Mercy Seat once a year.

The New Covenant brings finality to the old sacrifice system that is now obsolete, and if God doesn't recognize it any longer, those who are trying to establish their own self-righteousness by the law will experience outer darkness and gnash their teeth. There's no turning back to an old ritual system to relate with God our creator.

Romans 3:24 to 26 (King James Version) "Being justified freely by his grace through the redemption that is in Christ Jesus: Whom God has set forth to be a propitiation through faith in his blood, to declare his righteousness for the remission of sins that are past, through the forbearance of God; to declare, I say at this time his righteousness: that he might be the justifier of him which believeth In Jesus."

We can see clearly in this passage of scripture that God has been just to His own conscience concerning the sin of the individual who puts faith in the blood of Jesus that pays the ransom of their rebellious crimes against Him and His Kingdom. So right now this very second the blood of Jesus is speaking out on your behalf, cleansing you from failures, being free from an eternity of separation in hell, and including all the negative consequences from broken laws you have committed. God's very own righteousness being bestowed to the individual who personally believes in Jesus' work of redemption. You become the very righteousness of God in Christ (2 Corinthians 5:21).

Restitution for crimes committed in the physical world will most probably still be held against you and punishment given accordingly.

THE MERCY SEAT

Let's have a look back at what God told Moses while the law was the standard that prevailed in Exodus 25:22.

"There will I meet with thee, and I will commune with thee from above the Mercy Seat between the two cherubim which are upon the Ark of the Covenant."

Here's a glimpse of what's transpiring. The word propitiation means a mercy seat, a place where God turns His wrath away or judgment from the guilty, thereby stopping punishment. So sacrificial animal blood is sprinkled on the Mercy Seat, (I might add the sacrifice had to meet law requirements, which meant using the best lamb in your flock) which is the lid of the Ark of the Covenant and the guilt of sins committed for that year are covered. They are forgiven, but under the animal's blood, their guilty conscience is not washed clean. God's glory falls because the blood covers the broken laws, rebellion to His chosen leadership, and divine provision. He now can interact with the High Priest, who represents the nation.

NEW COVENANT REALITY

We now see Jesus as the present Mercy Seat. Christ now being the place where guilt and penalty are forgiven and the curse of the law broken and the blessing released. The throne of grace is Jesus, where God meets with the repentant sinner to establish a New Blood Covenant with each recipient. You will have a white stone with your name on it in Heaven that only you and Jesus know. He's going to keep it real and personal with you forever. His love never fails or ends! (Rev. 2:15) Jesus is now God's meeting place with man. It's not limited to a building with a bell.

In Romans 3:24, Paul uses the name Jesus Christ to refer to our Savior. It means the Anointed One, or the Exalted One who emptied Himself out. The suffering man on Earth, humiliated, a man of sorrow, and acquainted with grief. He was despised and rejected by His own creation.

FIRST HUMAN ENCOUNTER

In the gospel of John 20:11, 12 we read how Mary Magdalene, weeping, stooped down and looked into the tomb where Jesus had been laid and saw two angels in white sitting; the one at the head and the other at the feet where the corpse of the Savior had laid. What a symbolic picture of the Mercy Seat there in the tomb with the two winged cherubim as on the Ark of the Covenant. Mary then exits the tomb and encounters the risen Lamb of God. She doesn't recognize Jesus' new resurrected body. Most likely she wasn't expecting to encounter Him, already inferring that someone had removed the body from the sepulcher,. However there is no questioning the loving voice of the Master when He calls her name. Here's the reality: God meets Mary through and in Christ at His resurrection. Jesus is now the man in the glory, the Mercy Seat where we too obtain grace and forgiveness. An eternal release from the fear of death and separation from God. The recognized spiritual awareness that He's alive and I'm forgiven. Heaven's gates are open wide. The quickening when the Holy Spirit seals our spirit and we're born again. The point of conversion when we are now alive in Christ.

   1st John 17:5 "And now, O father, glorify thou me with thine own self with the glory which I had with thee before the world was."

THE ARK OF THE COVENANT

The Ark and how it's constructed points directly to Christ. It was made of shittim wood that refers to the created natural man, and then is overlaid with gold, that speaks to the divine. Here we see the two-fold duality of the Savior. Supernatural God in a mortal flesh body. Within the Ark itself were the tablets of the law (second edition), Aaron's budding staff that indicates divine leadership, God's choice of the anointed one, and finally hidden manna from Heaven that represents God's provision. All three categories or statutes broken by fallen humanity. Behold the Lamb of God slain before the foundation of the world, He is the only one to fulfill every requirement of the law, and was perfect in all His ways to be a substitution sacrifice for the sin of Adam's fall and yours. Jesus is everything represented in the Ark.

Another fact about the lid of the Ark is how the cherubim faced each other at each end of the Mercy Seat, their eyes fixed on the blood sprinkled there by the High Priest. It echoes the words spoken to Moses about the Passover blood on the door and lintel posts in Egypt, Exodus 12:13. "When I see the blood, I will pass over you, when I smite the land of Egypt."

Both are types and shadows of the Lord Jesus Christ. In the Old Covenant, God's forbearance overlooked the Jews that broke the law, rebellion to leadership and disregarded divine provision that was put under the sprinkled blood. Now He commands all men everywhere to repent. It can't be overstated that Jesus' blood removes our sin as far as the east is from the west. If you start on a journey going west young man, you'll never arrive in the east. Or if you go east, you'll never arrive in the west! In Christ God can't see through the blood of Jesus, or should I say there is no need to. Justification is accomplished when the blood is received and applied by childlike faith. Complete acquittal is the verdict, not a stay of execution till you clean up your life.

Revelation 12:11 "And they overcame him (the devil or Satan) by the blood of the Lamb, and the word of their testimony; and they loved not their selves unto death."

Post Script:

You have a testimony, so use some words and say something concerning the hope that lies within you about your eternal life in Heaven.

He carried the full weight
of your punishment,
tasting death for you
that included outer darkness,
the absence of God's light
and His love.

CHAPTER 17
The Veil Of The Most Holy Place

When Jesus yielded up his spirit, the veil in the temple at Jerusalem that hung before the Holy of Holies was torn from top to bottom. It consisted of two very heavy tapestries hung with an eighteen-inch space between them separating the Hekhal, Holy Place, and the Devir, the Most Holy Place where the Ark of the Covenant was located. Hebrews 9:23, 24 gives us a reference point to a comparison between the physical veil and earthly temple and the veil and the temple in Heaven today.

Verse 23 "It was therefore necessary that the copies (on earth) of things in the heavens should be cleansed with these; (the sprinkling of sacrificial blood verses 21, 22) but the heavenly things themselves with better sacrifices than these."

Verse 24 "For Christ is not entered into the holy places made with hands, which are the examples of the real one; but into Heaven itself, now to appear in the presence of God for us."

Once and for all He has taken away the first Covenant of the law to establish the new and living blood Covenant.

In Hebrews 10:20, that we have boldness to enter the holiest place by the blood of Jesus, by a new and living way which he has prepared for us, through the veil, that is to say, His flesh.

This is a relevant point because it reinforces the deity of Jesus, and the radical violent end to the Old Covenant and the introduction to the new.

We see the first glimpse of God's power in Christ at his baptism when the Holy Spirit falls on Him like a cloud described as a dove. Then again, on the Mount of Transfiguration, with Moses and Elias, when the glory of God did shine as the sun from Jesus' face and his raiment was white as light. It's true the glory rested on Moses after his mountain experience receiving the Ten Commandments, but it paled and faded away.

Just as the law and its glory has. Jesus, the only begotten son of God, manifested the unmeasurable glory of his Father, full of grace and truth. His flesh was the veil between us and the supernatural power of God's Kingdom that resided within Him.

Colossians 2:9 "For in him dwelleth all the fullness of the God Head bodily, and you are complete in him, which is the head of all rule and authority and power."

The exclamation point the disciples had was God's own direction to them, "This is my beloved son in whom I am well pleased; hear him." (Matthew 17:5) Jesus also said if you have seen me you have seen the Father, and, "My doctrine is not my own but He who has sent me." Jesus' incarnate body was the veil between God and His creation. This allowed God to display His love for mankind, to touch, embrace, heal, and forgive.

Jesus went into the most holy place in heaven, the very throne room of God, and presented his blood before his Father on your behalf. The Lord sitting on His throne, high and lifted up, with His train filling the temple. Six winged seraphim above God crying out to one another, "Holy, holy, holy is the Lord of hosts; the whole earth is filled with His Glory, and pillars shaking with the glory cloud like smoke filling the room." (Isaiah 6:1-4)

In conclusion, the physical veil in the copied temple on earth was only opened once a year. It's gone now, a fallen replica of a discarded worship system of laws and ordinances. Jesus has opened up the throne room in Heaven, giving us direct entrance to interact with the creator of all things. Personal relationship with Father God who gives us breath.

Christ has become our High Priest, who lives forever to make intercession for his people. He has replaced the priesthood office with Himself. Our New Blood Covenant, the last will and Testament of Jesus our mediator whose blood sprinkled in Heaven, speaks better things than that of Abel's that cried from the ground. Christ's blood speaks Luke (4:18), forgiveness and restoration with God, healing of the brokenhearted, deliverance to the captives, recovery of sight to the blind, to set at liberty those who are oppressed. (see Chapter 9, page 38)

CHAPTER 18

First Fruit From The Grave

When Jesus destroyed the authority of Satan in his death, burial, and resurrection, he legally confiscated the keys of Hades and death. He then did not rise from the grave alone.

Revelation 1:17, 18 "Fear not; I am the first and the last. I am he that liveth, and was dead; and behold I am alive forever, amen and have the keys of hell and death."

A SECOND EXODUS

There were other events occurring along with earthquakes, splitting of rocks in Jerusalem the morning the stone rolled away, and Jesus burst forth in glorious victory from the tomb.

Many bodies of the saints who previously died were

raised also and went into the holy city appearing to many.

Matthew 27:52-54 "And the graves were opened; and many bodies of the saints which were dead, and came out of the graves after his resurrection, and went into the holy city, and appeared unto many."

That would have been quite an astonishing encounter to be face-to-face with a formerly dead loved one or neighbor you knew in the past. Maybe these who engaged the newly risen had been to their funerals. We can probably think of someone even now dear to our heart that's passed, and we would love to see again. Great news if you're both in Christ – you most certainly will! Isaiah had something to say about it.

Isaiah 26:19 "Your dead shall live, together with my dead body they shall arise. Awake and sing, you who dwell in the dust; for your dew is like the dew of herbs, and the earth shall cast out the dead."

THE DECLARATION IN HADES

As I prayerfully meditated on these scriptures, I couldn't help but focus on the parable that Jesus taught in Luke 16:19-31. The rich man and Lazarus. As you may remember, Lazarus had a very difficult life, and the rich man lacked any compassion during his. Both suffered death, and the angels carried Lazarus to Abraham's bosom.

Bosom means a place of rest or a mattress where comfort is found and your needs are met, a safe, protected location. Not sure if it's firm or soft, but a whole lot better than where the rich man ended up.

Scripture says the rich man was buried and lifted up his eyes being tormented and saw Lazarus in Abraham's bosom and cried out for mercy. It's interesting that the rich man isn't given a name, but he represents people who have no compassion. I would associate him with the lust of the flesh, lust of the eyes, and the pride of life bunch.

The rich man can see Lazarus in Abraham's bosom. There must have been water there. He's desperate for just a drop of water due to his suffering in the flames. He requests Abraham to send Lazarus to quench his thirst. Shoe's on the other foot now.

The rich man still sees Lazarus as subservient.

Point to ponder: Jesus said the greatest among you

shall be a servant. Even if Lazarus wanted to take water to the rich man, he could not, due to the protective gulf fixed between the two, stopping passage to and fro.

The rich man's second request is to send Lazarus to warn his five brothers so they could escape this place of suffering. Abraham replies that they have Moses and the prophets, let them heed them.

The rich man's third appeal is to send one back from the dead, for surely they will repent. Again, Abraham's answer is the prophetic word of the Old Covenant and the law of Moses.

WHO'S IN THERE?

Well, we know Abraham is present, he is the individual God cut the Old Blood Covenant with. Those found to be faithful under the law are present. We are surrounded by a great cloud of witnesses. In Hebrews 11:13-40, these verses describe to us the Old Testament believers who obtained a good testimony through faith and died having not received the promise of Messiah. God's appointed time for Jesus' incarnation had not yet come. So those of whom the world considers not worthy are there. Would God let their spirits wait with the wicked? Absolutely not. Nor would Jesus leave them behind when he rose from the dead.

The scriptures clearly tell us Jesus preached to the spirits of the dead. Their physical bodies are gone, but their spirits are alive, not asleep in the grave. Two portions of scripture theologians wrestle with are the point of the next few paragraphs.

1 Peter 3:19 "By whom also he went and preached to the spirits in prison. Who formerly were disobedient, when once the divine long-suffering waited in the days of Noah, while the ark was being prepared, in which a few, that is eight souls, were saved through water."

The circumstance of the flood, the ark, and its occupants, formed a type, and baptism that forms a corresponding type. Each setting forth the spiritual realities of the death, burial, and resurrection of believers in their identification with Christ. It is not just washing away the filth of the flesh, but the key is a cleansed good conscience. Scripture is very clear that only the blood of Jesus can cleanse a guilty conscience. While water is an outward obedience to declare before men your identification with Jesus, it does not remit your sins. Baptism can be just another self-righteous effort to merit right standing with God and apart from genuine faith will just render the participant wet, their destination to Hell or Hades unchanged.

Hebrews 9:14 "How much more shall the blood of Christ, who through the eternal spirit offered himself without spot to God, cleanse your conscience from dead works to serve the living God."

To those people who were faithful in life, the entrance of their spirits to Heaven has just been declared to them by their long-awaited Messiah!

The second scripture:

1 Peter 4:6 "For this reason the gospel was preached also to those who are dead, that they might be judged according to men in the flesh, but live according to God in the spirit."

Because God takes no joy in the judgment of the wicked, there is still the need for righteousness to be established. Those who had done evil in His sight and weren't repentant in the flesh were doomed to their fate. They were not given a second chance to repent but finality of why they wouldn't be released with those in Abraham's bosom, that had been faithful to God in their physical bodies.

Here are two examples of where our spirit goes after physical death. The thief on the cross who asks Jesus to, "Remember me when you come into your kingdom." Jesus replies, "Today you will be with me in paradise."

The believing criminal couldn't just pass Abraham's bosom and go straight to Heaven, because the work of the redemption took three days. His spirit went to Abraham's bosom and exited with Jesus at His resurrection.

The second example is now during the dispensation of grace by faith.

Hebrews 12:22, 23 "This verse tells us that when we approach Mount Zion, the city of the living God, Heavenly Jerusalem, there is an innumerable company of Angels, the general assembly and the Church of the first born, who are registered in Heaven, to God the judge of all and to the spirits of just men made perfect."

We can see clearly that redeemed spirits of men without a resurrected physical body are present in Heaven now. Paul said to be absent from the body is to be present with the Lord. With a clear conscience, without feelings of inferiority and false guilt, they stand before their loving Heavenly Father. The blood of Jesus washes white as snow.

A VICTORY PARADE

It is a proven historical truth that when the Roman Legion destroyed their enemy, they had a royal procession to their city of origin. On display were the captive kings and court, wise men and counselors as well as those to be slaves, the seized riches of gold, silver and precious gems. Many times the thumbs of any who might be a threat were cut off so they could never grip a weapon against Rome again.

Jesus had his own parade as He burst forth, destroying death, sickness, hell, and the grave. There was a host of angelic praise and rays of light flashing to the sky as Christ pierced through the darkness, cutting away and disarming rulers of darkness and displacing powers from authority in an open display of God's power. Triumphing over the wicked demonic foe at the cross, displaying victory in His resurrection. Colossians 2:15 King James Version "And having spoiled principalities and powers, he made a shew of them openly, triumphing over them in it, through His cross."

You have a blood covenant privilege
to receive your inheritance
in Christ.

CHAPTER 19

The Accession Of Redemption

The last task Jesus had to accomplish for us was to present Himself before almighty God as that new and living sacrifice by presenting his blood on the heavenly altar. In approaching this final act of our provision for salvation, we'll need to attempt to understand why Christ must purify the tabernacle or temple in Heaven and what that involved.

Hebrews New King James Version 9:20-24 This portion of scripture starts with the description of Moses according to the law purifying the people, books, tabernacle and all the vessels of the ministry with sprinkled animal blood.

20: Moses speaking, "This is the blood of the covenant which God has commanded you."

21: "Then, likewise, he sprinkled with blood both the tabernacle and all the vessels of the ministry."

22: "And according to the law almost all things are purified with blood, and without shedding of blood there is no remission."

23: "Therefore it was necessary that the copies of the things in the Heavens should be purified with these, but the Heavenly things themselves with better sacrifices than these."

24: "For Christ has not entered the Holy place made with hands, which are copies of the true, but into heaven itself, now to appear in the presence of God for us."

Verses 23 and 24 draw a direct parallel between two different tabernacles, one on earth, a copy, and the real Temple in Heaven where God dwells. Obviously, the life of Jesus' carnate body was in his blood and was perfect as discussed in an earlier chapter, thereby being the acceptable offering that more than satisfied God's wrath.

THE HEAVENLY TABERNACLE PURIFIED

I asked myself why and how the temple in heaven became defiled. I contacted a number of colleagues and friends whose opinions I trust. Whose lives, I might add, express upright spiritual character, and of course who hold to good sound doctrine. Some of these friends are pastors, missionaries, evangelists, and Bible college administrators.

How did Adam's sin reach into the heavens and bring defilement to God's temple? What a loaded question or spiritual curve ball I pitched at them! Of all the responses I received, the most significant was, "How would this truth help believers walk in the peace and love of God, to fulfill His will in their lives and, above all, to walk in the spirit?"

My first thought was – I hadn't thought of that at all. I'll give my answer in the chapter conclusion.

A HOLY TEMPLE

The first step to take in answering this question is to define what makes a temple. Who makes a temple holy? Jesus had a few things to discuss with the scribes and Pharisees over their hypocrisies. In Matthew 23:16-23 the conversation turns to the temple and what constitutes a man keeping his word when he swears an oath. Swearing by the temple or its gold, altar or the gift. Jesus sums up the truth, "Which is greater, the gift or the altar that sanctifies the gift? He who swears by the temple swears by it and by Him who dwells in it. And he who swears by heaven swears by the throne of God and by Him who sits on it."

So our Heavenly Father dwells in His temple, and He alone makes it Holy by his presence. Furthermore, the binding obligation to keep ones' word is never to be taken idly, knowing an accounting of every word will be judged for those not in Christ (Matthew 12:36).

God Himself was offended with Adam's sin in the garden, and his forfeiting the authority and standing he had held in the heavens.

Romans 5:17 "For if by the one man's offense death reigned through the one, much more those who receive abundance of grace and of the gift of righteousness will reign in life through the one, Jesus Christ."

It is clear to see that the offense affected Heaven and the temple. Adam broke his relationship with God and brought death to the new creation.

Adam was God's physical representative on earth to manage this new world, and was in co-leadership that give him legitimacy before God on earth as in Heaven. God the Father would leave His throne to come and walk and fellowship with Adam in the cool of the day. They hung out together.

The offense to love fractured and broke the relationship between God and this newly created man, causing enmity between the two. With the relationship defiled, and trust wounded, the result now has reached the temple and God's heart. God is love. He is holy and will not fellowship with evil, so the new couple is removed. Even the goodness of the Tree of the Knowledge of Good and Evil will not sustain a relationship with the Holiness of God the Father.

The knowledge of goodness from the tree cannot discern the divinity of God, and He will not fellowship with evil or its presence.

THE SUPPLANTER

It is clear that Satan's rebellion was the forerunner to Adam's disobedience. His arrogance caused his expulsion from Heaven to crawl on his belly as a snake on earth. This personifies his wickedness, evil intentions to kill and destroy humanity. Satan mounted a counter-attack against God through his new created man. Adam loses his legal authority and forfeits it by default through deception. Satan now has attained a false but recognized authority by God.

Luke 10:18 Jesus speaking, "I saw Satan fall like lightning from Heaven."

Isaiah 14:12 New King James "How you are fallen from Heaven, O Lucifer, son of the morning! How you are cut down to the ground."

Job chapter one gives us new insight on how devastating Adam's fall was. Satan had been cast out of Heaven but we see him back in the presence of God boasting of his new acquisition of earth and its inhabitants. The fall has given him new access through Adam's lost authority. He came as God's adversary to create trouble, accusation, the hater of all that's good before God's throne.

Job 1:7a, "And the Lord said to Satan, 'From where do you come?' So Satan answered the Lord and said,

'From going to and fro on the earth, and from walking back and forth on it.'"

1 Peter 5:8 "Be sober, be vigilant because your adversary the devil walks about like a roaring lion, seeking whom he may devour."

The father of lies is taunting his creator with his power over earth, and he can't find anyone faithful to God. II Corinthians 4:4 tells us that Satan is the god of this world who blinds the minds of those who believe not the glorious Gospel of Christ. This is still going on in your neighborhood today.

Remember Jesus' wilderness temptation. Satan offered him all the kingdoms of the world if he would worship him. How could he offer them if he didn't control them at that time? (Luke 4:1-11)

Ephesians 6 also tells us we fight against the wiles of the devil, "principalities and powers, rulers of darkness of this fallen world, against spiritual wickedness in high places."

Satan has the keys to Hades and Death. We have already discussed in previous chapters that now our enemy has been disarmed, his authority nullified for the saints. The Pentagon of Hell has been obliterated through Christ's atoning work at Calvary. If we'll choose to walk in love and the power of the Holy Spirit, our enemies will be thrown into a confused state of disarray.

Jesus sent 70 others out with power over all the enemies, and nothing would by any means harm them.

Luke 10:19: "Behold I give you the authority to trample on serpents and scorpions, and over all the power of the enemy and nothing shall by any means hurt you."

These 70 others are not part of the twelve. We have settled for a gospel message that pales of the original message of the kingdom of God. We need a desperate return to a message of power that God can again work with us with signs and wonders confirming the preaching of His Word. To be trained and understand the authority of the believer to accomplish God's plans and his purposes on earth, and not our 501(c)3 corporate agendas. "'Not by might nor by power but by my Spirit,' says the Lord, who alone is worthy of all honor and praise."

I've personally seen God do all manner of miracles, signs, and wonders in every nation He has sent me to. Deaf ears opened, stroke victims running down church aisles, epileptics healed and demons cast out, cancer healed. When you get to heaven, you can rent the DVD if you're of a mind to. Only in the West have we labored so hard to discredit what Jesus has paid in full for, complete redemption. We take no personal responsibility for our spiritual maturity. Whatever will be will be. It seems a hyper sovereignty of God teaching has come from the book of Job and has not submitted itself to the death, burial, and resurrection of Jesus. There seems to be only a title page in the Bible between the old and new covenant.

NO ADMITTANCE

Some still hold fast to the book of Job that Satan still comes before God to bring accusation against you. That era is over! He will get nowhere. The blood of Jesus is still speaking on your behalf in heaven.

Hebrews 12:24 "To Jesus the Mediator of the New Covenant, and to the blood of sprinkling that speaks better things than that of Abel."

Abel's blood cried out of vengeance. Jesus' blood calls for mercy and forgiveness. Furthermore, all the laws you've broken have been blotted out by this blood and there's no record of your sin in the memory file of God! (Colossians 2:3)

"As we are walking in the light we have fellowship with one another and God. There is a continual cleansing by the blood of Jesus Christ (1 John 1:7). It is not by the performance and religious law or traditions of men.

The only scripture on this side of redemption that remotely resembles a direct satanic confrontation dealing with a human's body or sin is found in Jude, verse 9. This letter deals primarily with apostates that have perverted the Gospel message. A comparison is made of Michael the Archangel and these brute beasts who reject God and all authority. Here, when the devil was contending with Michael over the body of Moses, he didn't bring reviling accusations against the enemy but said, "The Lord rebuke you!"

What I see here is, if Satan could still go before the throne in heaven, why fight with an angel when you can attack God on his throne in heaven? I'll tell you why: he can't! He's no longer allowed to come before God to get permission to attack the saints. We are redeemed through faith in Christ Jesus who has paid our debt of sin. It's not based on our compliance with the law. We already have failed at our own attempts to justify ourselves. Some still believe the devil is God's errand boy, doing his dirty work on earth. Satan is a defeated foe. Jesus told us he comes to kill steal and destroy, John 10:10. What part of that picture doesn't the church get? Our heavenly Father gets all the blame for what Satan gets away with because we won't make a stand or fight the fight of faith.

We are to submit ourselves to God, resist the devil, and he will flee. I didn't say it was easy. Paul told Timothy to:

1 Timothy 6:12 "Fight the good fight of faith, lay hold on eternal life, to which you were also called and have confessed the good confession in the presence of many witnesses."

There's never a victory without a fight. No testimony without a test. He won't visit your house if he knows he'll be cut up by the Sword of the Spirit, beat up with the name above all names and hogtied with the blood. The weapons of our warfare are not carnal but mighty to the pulling down of strongholds, casting out demons and healing the sick!

Jude verse 9 is referenced to Zechariah 3:2, where the Angel of the Lord rebukes Satan, who stands to oppose Joshua the high priest in this vision. "And the Lord said to Satan, 'The Lord rebuke you, Satan.'"

We have already looked at who the Angel of the Lord is, the incarnate Christ. Reinforced again by the text the Lord said, clearly telling us it is not just an angel, but the Angel of the Lord, Yahweh. The Archangel Michael follows Christ's pre-incarnate example. It's time for the Church to rise up and use her authority!

CONCLUSION

Here's my conclusion on the question of the Heavenly Temple. First of all, it is God Himself who sanctifies the temple. When He is not satisfied that justice has been served, there is no peace with his creation. After our justification through faith in Christ Jesus' blood and its presence in heaven speaking on our behalf, the wall of division has been removed, opening up relationship again as in the garden of Eden before the knowledge of good and evil destroyed pure fellowship.

Satan is now thrown down and no longer controls the converted believer wiout their invitation nor can bring accusations to God in Heaven. ("My children are taken captive by lack of knowledge." Hosea 4:6) He does lie to us to bring us under condemnation or to turn us against our brothers and sisters in Christ. Quit listening! Believe what the Word says about you.

Jesus is sitting on the right hand of God till all his enemies are put under his feet. He is now our High Priest that ever liveth to make intercession on our behalf.

We are legal citizens of heaven, with our names written in the Lamb's Book of Life. Just as important is the fact that we have been adopted into God's family, becoming his very own children, whereby we can call him Abba.

Romans 8:15 "For you did not receive the spirit of

bondage again to fear, but you received the spirit of adoption by whom we cry out, 'Abba Father!'"

CHAPTER 20
The Reveal

Jesus pursued two distraught disciples on their seven-mile trip to the village of Emmaus. He drew near to the wayward, who did not believe the women of their company that followed Jesus. They had heard their testimony of finding his tomb empty and then having encountered a vision of angels declaring Jesus was alive.

We know only one name of the two was Cleopas. Jesus doesn't reveal himself at first but invites himself into their grieving conversation about his crucifixion and death. They saw him as only a prophet, mighty in deed and word before God and all the people, but not the Son of God, the long-awaited Messiah.

Jesus goes back in history to expound the scriptures concerning himself. Faith comes by hearing and hearing by the word of God. They had a first-row seat during Jesus' ministry and still didn't comprehend who he was and his mission of redemption.

Jesus, speaking in Luke 24:25-26:

"O foolish ones, and slow of heart to believe in all that the prophets have spoken! Ought not the Christ to have suffered these things and to enter into his glory?"

COVENANT MEAL

Eternal life is walking down a dusty road revealing himself through the Word, and then Jesus pretends to indicate he will continue his journey on past Emmaus, all the while knowing their hearts are his targeted destination. The Holy Spirit is drawing and burning in their hearts, and they compel Jesus to stay with them. It's late in the day and beginning to get dark.

It still seems as though the principality of the air is still blinding their eyes from the truth. When they sat down to eat a meal together, Jesus, as he had countless times before, blessed the food with them, took the bread in hand, and breaking it revealed the scars of the driven nails. Their eyes are spiritually opened, and they know him. Jesus vanished from their physical sight. Jesus wanted them to pursue him, but it's not nearly as much as he desires communion with them or you and I. He leaves the 99 sheep and comes after us.

Revelation 3:20

"Behold I stand at the door and knock. If anyone hears my voice and opens the door I will come into him and dine with him, and he with me."

This is a picture of a blood covenant meal within the heart and spirit of the converted. True fellowship with the Godhead is within us. Jesus is saying by the Holy Spirit I will come into you and you in me. Christ in us, the Hope of Glory!

You can partake of the bread and wine but have no communion with God the Father and Jesus. Don't let the cares of this world choke out intimacy with your true love.

KNOWN BY THE SCARS

In chapter 4, "Cutting A Blood Covenant," we discussed six possible steps that were integrated into the pagan ceremony. We see two taking place in this passage of scripture. One, the covenant meal also personified in the Last Supper, but in this case, both a physical and spiritual communion.

Second, although not written in this passage, the covenant known by the scars of Jesus' crucifixion. No question about the revealing to Thomas or the disciples in the locked room in John 20:20, 27-29.

"You are blessed who have not seen and yet believe."

John 20:20, 27 "'Peace be with you.' When he had said this, he showed them his hands and his side. Then the disciples were glad when they saw the Lord. 'Reach your finger here, and look at my hands, and reach your hand here, and put it into my side. Do not be unbelieving, but believing.'"

Jesus wasn't willing to lose Thomas. On the contrary, he made a special trip just to reveal himself to him. He won't abandon you when you doubt during dark trials of grief and suffering. He will confirm his love. Keep standing. The light has not left you! Love will never fail.

Cleopas and his companion did a complete u-turn in their lives. Emmaus had no hold on their regenerated spirits. They rose up that very hour and returned to

Jerusalem, where they found the eleven and witnessed to them, "The Lord is risen indeed."

Spiritually, we, as believers, can find ourselves wandering down a lane that is leading us away from God's will and his best for our life. But we can turn around! Just one encounter can change your destination. Put on your flashers and pull over. Return to your first love. Go do the things you formerly did when your passion burned for Christ. Lukewarm is not going to keep you happy! Look up! The fields are still white unto harvest!

Luke 14:23

"Then the Master said to the servant, 'Go out into the highways and hedges, and compel them to come in, that my house may be filled.'"

Let the love of God compel you with the hope that lies within you. That happens only when you're led by the spirit of love. People are groping in the darkness for truth in a world that's upside down. Let the spirit blow on your wick till the candle flame in your heart becomes ablaze!

CHAPTER 21

Where's That Coupon?

I had a funny experience last week when I went to redeem a coupon. It was worth $3 on a haircut. I certainly don't want to trivialize the word "redeem," a serious theological term, but give a practical example of its definition.

This particular day I had a number of errands to run. One thing on the list was a haircut. I was getting woolly around the ears.

I arrived at my destination, wondering who might try to scalp me that day. I waited about 15 minutes. I got my new do, participated in some chit chat, then proceeded to the register to pay my bill.

I told the gal who did the snipping that I had a coupon, but lo and behold – it wasn't in my pocket or my wallet. Now, $3 wasn't going to break the bank, but

I had taken time to cut that bugger out, and now my plan was foiled.

I paid the full price measured against me. There was no pity from the business owner, who might have pulled out a coupon and given it to me. My tough luck, that wasn't happening.

When I returned home, I found the coupon was right on the kitchen table where I had left it.

I had every intention of redeeming the value the coupon provided. It was mailed to me, offered, and I possessed it. I simply neglected to pay attention so I could exchange it for the savings. So I went without. I laughed a bit, then threw the coupon away. The date would expire before I could redeem it for another haircut.

As I contemplated this experience, the Holy Spirit started talking to me about it.

Galatians 3:13 "Christ has redeemed us from the curse of the law, being made a curse for us: for it is written cursed is every one that hangs on a tree (Deuteronomy 23:23)."

Colossians 1:14 "In whom (Jesus) we have redemption through his blood, even the forgiveness of sins."

Colossians 1:19, 20 "For it pleased the Father that in him should all fullness dwell; and having made peace through the blood of his cross, by him to unite all things unto himself; whether they be things in earth, or things in Heaven."

Jesus was the divine coupon that is still redeemable today. He humbled himself, became a man and walked among his creation, which received him not, and paid the ultimate price for you. He completed the will of His Father. Didn't pass the cup of suffering so peace could be established, restoration within a loving relationship. Rules and law do not produce relationship. God puts his highest value on relationship with you. I'll close with this scripture.

Romans 8:31, 32 "What shall we say to these things? If God is for us who can be against us? He that spared not his own son, but delivered him up for us all, how shall he not with him also freely give us all things?"

Redeem your coupon. What else do you need? Your Daddy God loves you!

Until you understand
what your legal inheritance is,
you'll never believe or receive it.
It is not dispersed randomly,
but according to your revelation of it,
and child-like confidence.

CHAPTER 22

Benefits Of The Blood

Throughout this book, I have shared different aspects of Christ's redeeming work for our lives, and the power of His blood to saturate the content with God's grace and mercy.

The final chapters will deal directly with the benefits of faith in Christ and his blood that cut the New Blood Covenant.

THE NEW TESTAMENT VS. THE OLD

I heard a young senior pastor teach that the only difference between the covenants was there now was no need for circumcision. Clearly, that was evidence of a lack of understanding of his redemption. Let's compare the major points.

A. Cutting the Old Covenant; God clearly had

no blood to shed on the divine side to consecrate the ceremony. So Abram provided the animals and sacrificed them. Then God walked between the split animal halves. Abraham received circumcision as a shedding of blood and sign of the covenant with God. The laws were given under Moses to force obedience to God and proper interaction with the populace.

B. The New Covenant; Jesus shed his blood for us, and we have the circumcision of the heart (Colossians 3:11) that is described in Hebrews 4:12. We shed no blood and have no scars to reflect our covenant, but God's laws are now written on the tablets of our hearts, and we are a new creation. We could not perform the law with perfection and could not reverse the fall of Adam that brought death to us. Jesus fulfilled all the law requirements and was sacrificed for us and defeated death by resurrection from the dead. He translated us out of the Kingdom of darkness into the Kingdom of the Son of His love (Colossians 1: 13,14). "The sting of death is sin, and the strength of sin is the law." 1 Corinthians 15:56

FREE FROM PERFORMANCE OF THE LAW

To free us from condemnation, God removed the law that empowers sin over our lives. The sting of death is fear of rejection by God or damnation. When you know you're forgiven, the condemnation of failure to keep all the law must go. So God has freed us from the law of sin and death.

Romans 3:27 "Where is the boasting then? It is excluded. By what law? Of works? No, by the law of faith. Therefore we conclude that a man is justified by faith apart from the deeds of the law."

Romans 8:1-2 "There is therefore now no condemnation to those who are in Christ Jesus, who do not walk according to the flesh, but according to the Spirit."

Galatians 5:16 "Walk in the spirit and you will not fulfill the lust of the flesh. (17) For the flesh lusts against the Spirit, and the Spirit against the flesh, and these are contrary to one another so that you do not do the things that you wish. (18) But if you are led by the Spirit, you are not under the law."

We are now under the law of the spirit of life in

Christ Jesus and the law of faith that set us free from the law of sin and death (Romans 8:2).

I think it's imperative that we yield to the spirit of life in us. After all, He is trying to help us on a daily basis. The Holy Spirit is the one who conveys the wisdom, the answers you need for family, business, direction, encouragement and on and on. He is the spirit of truth. The Holy Spirit knows everything! He's a genius.

We know that the just will live by faith and whatsoever is not of faith is sin. Enjoy your salvation; be free. The Holy Spirit will convict you if you're doing something wrong. He doesn't condemn, that's the work of the law and the accuser, Satan. Being rebuked by the Holy Spirit is a good thing. We always need to re-adjust and apologize to our Father and those we offend.

Think about this point: You're cursed if you can't continue in all things which are written in the book of the law. This type of mixed message brings confusion and a sin conscience, not a clear conscience to serve the living God. (Hebrews 9:14)

Galatians 3:11, 12 "But that no one is justified by the law in the sight of God is evident, for the just shall live by faith. Yet the law is not of faith, but the man who does them shall live by them."

Christ has already redeemed us from the curse of the law, having become a curse for us by being hung on a tree. The main theme of the epistle to the Galatian believers is salvation by faith alone.

Here are a few more verses on this subject to study: Romans 7:6; Romans 6:7; 2 Corinthians 3:9; Romans 8:4.

ONLY ONE GOSPEL

Paul addressed false teachers that were perverting the truth with law and performance of works of the flesh for salvation.

Galatians 1: 6, 7 "I marvel that you are turning away so soon from Him who called you in the grace of Christ, to a different gospel. Which is not another; but there are some who trouble you and want to pervert the Gospel of Christ."

You will not receive the sealing work of the Holy Spirit or His filling for power by mixing the Gospel with laws (Ephesians 1:13, Acts 1:8).

Human effort is the foundation of all cults to achieve whatever their deceptive spiritual motivation is comprised of.

Galatians 3:1, 2 "O foolish Galatians! Who has bewitched you that you should not obey the truth, before whose eyes Jesus Christ was clearly portrayed among you as crucified? This only I want to learn of you: Did you receive the spirit by the works of the law, or by the hearing of faith? Are you so foolish? Having begun in the Spirit, are you now being made perfect by the flesh?"

The question I most often heard when I was traveling abroad was: "Why doesn't God do miracles in America?" My answer: "He does miracles where he can."

Galatians 3:5 "Therefore, He (God) who supplies the spirit to you and works miracles among you, does he do it by the works of the law, or by the hearing of faith?"

This is a major problem when most want to have their ears tickled and work out their needs through fleshly means. Our own pride (the old man) keeps raising up against the Lordship of Christ in our lives.

The Israelites have a zeal for God, but it's not according to knowledge.

Romans 10:3, 4 "For they, being ignorant of God's righteousness, and seeking to establish their own righteousness, have not submitted to the righteousness of God. For Christ is the end of the law for righteousness to everyone who believes."

God's purpose is that we serve him in love from a pure heart, from a good conscience, and from sincere faith. Teachers of the law don't even understand what they say or what they affirm.

1 Timothy 1:8 "But we know that the law is good if one uses it lawfully or as it is intended under the New Covenant."

The law is not made for a righteous person (in Christ), but for the lawless and insubordinate, for the ungodly and for sinners, the unholy and profane, murderers of fathers and mothers, manslayers, fornicators, sodomites, kidnappers, liars, perjurers. And if there is any other wrong that is contrary to sound doctrine. I think the law in this instance is wonderful to protect civilization and to use to persuade the lost of their need for a savior.

THE GIVING OF GIFTS

Another practice was the giving of gifts to one another during the covenant ceremony. Eternal salvation will always be the most major gift you'll ever receive! It takes a lifetime on earth just to begin to unwrap and walk in newness of life in Christ. By the way, every good gift, every perfect gift, comes down from the Father of lights! How about the comforter? God sent us the Holy Spirit and the gifts he distributes in the body of Christ in 1 Corinthians 12:8-10. Also the ministry positions: apostles, prophets, evangelists, pastors, and teachers.

Ephesians 4:8 "When he ascended on high, he led captivity captive, and gave gifts to men."

If you faint in the day of adversity,
your strength is small.
Jesus is not weak,
so rest in Him under
His wings of protection!

"The name of the Lord
is like a high tower,
the righteous shall run in
and be safe." Proverbs 18:10

CHAPTER 23

Jesus' Blood: A Weapon

I mentioned in an earlier chapter the weapons of our warfare, so I want to examine the blood of Jesus and its significance as a weapon in the arsenal of the believer today. Here's a brief list that indicates our position of authority in Christ through his atoning blood.

YOUR POSITION IN CHRIST

1. We have overcome the evil one by the blood of the Lamb and the word of our testimony (Revelation 12:11).

2. We were translated out of the kingdom of darkness into the kingdom of his dear son. We now have redemption through his blood, the forgiveness of sins (Colossians 1:13, 14).

3. Jesus' blood does protect us in our sin as in Egypt, like lamb's blood applied to the doorposts and

mantels, but also removes, cleanses our rebellion and restores us to fellowship with God. It takes away the Passover law and creates a new spirit and clean conscience for service to the living God (Hebrews 9:14).

4. We have boldness in Christ to approach the throne of grace to obtain grace and mercy, finding help in time of need (Hebrews 4:16).

5. The blood of Jesus is speaking on our behalf in the heavenly temple of God. MERCY (Hebrews 12:24).

6. Blood flowed from the lacerations cut deep by the whip tipped with metal balls and sharp bone as Jesus paid for our physical afflictions and emotional torment (Isaiah 53 and 1 Peter 2:24). Our atonement and healing are linked together, and both are received by simple faith.

7. Jesus' blood gives us spiritual authority, of which most know very little about.

Mark 16:15-18 "Go ye into all the world and preach the Gospel to every creature. He that believeth and is baptized shall be saved, but he that believeth not shall be damned. And these signs shall follow them that believe; in my name shall they cast out devils, they shall speak with new tongues, they shall take up serpents and if they drink any deadly thing, it shall not hurt them, they shall lay hands on the sick and they shall recover."

I'm just hitting a few of the main points here, but I want to emphasize some things I've learned and experienced in the traveling ministry as well as normal life and the fight against the enemy hordes that come to steal, kill and destroy (John 10:10).

SUBMISSION: THE KEY TO AUTHORITY

In the book of Job, we see he was protected by a hedge of thorns that kept Satan and his not-so-merry spirits from attacking. In the New Covenant, under the work of Christ's redemption, we are told to submit ourselves to God, resist Satan, and any demonic presence, and they will flee. The Word, the name, and the blood are all powerful offensive weapons and are not in competition with each other. They, however, need to be skillfully used! The weapon of the blood is what I'm going to focus on.

As in the Old Testament, sacrificial blood was shed, and the glory of God's presence would fall. Mount

Carmel is a good example with Elijah. The declaration of the blood of Jesus by faith will manifest the Holy Spirit and angelic assistance! Praying and pleading the bloodline of protection is paramount when ministering deliverance to captives and healing to the afflicted. Just a quick note, when you're working extensively within gypsy ghettos, the enemy can manifest at any time in a person. You must be instant in season and out of season (2 Timothy 4:2). If God has sent you, Jesus will get the job done through you.

STUDY TO SHOW YOURSELF APPROVED

I was led to begin studying about the blood of Jesus in the late 80's and right on till now. I'll share a number of personal testimonies, but I want to start with one of the first testimonies I read about that began to build my faith in this area of warfare.

PLEADING AND PRAYING THE BLOODLINE

Pleading in this aspect is more a legal term like pleading a case in a courtroom. You are stating your position in Christ based on Biblical truth, not begging in fear.

This testimony is about a minister and his wife, who were invited to Canada to hold revival meetings.

God was moving powerfully and there were many converts along with deliverances from all types of bondages. I would say hell was shrinking and heaven was expanding. It had to be powerful enough to get Satan's attention because he threatened the evangelist that he would kill his children with foxes that had rabies in the woods near their rural Tennessee home if he continued the ministry. He recalled his neighbor's reports of having seen foxes in the area. Just like the devil to attack with fear. The evangelist rebuked Satan and gathered with three other believers. With simple faith they prayed a bloodline around the property line of his land. The ministry continued. The following week he received news in a letter from his brother that five dead foxes had been found along his Tennessee property line. The heads were removed and tested positive for rabies. Satan sent them; the bloodline killed them. Praise God! There's power in the blood of Jesus to save, protect, heal, and deliver! (Testimony of Don Gossett, Praise Avenue, Box 2, Blaine, Washington)

    A colleague and I were in Transylvania, Romania, and ministering in several towns and staying in the village of Voslobeani. I had an invitation to minister in a spirit-filled church in Sighisoara. It was a very cold winter day, and we were traveling through the mountains on not the best roads. The car heater was poor – no, it was terrible! As we descended down into a valley, we were leaving one province, Harghita, and entering another. Out in the middle of nowhere was a police checkpoint. Pastor Fere Gego was stopped, and the car and his papers were checked out until they could manufacture a fine. Within the next three-fourths mile, we were spiritually attacked. Some of the most wicked thoughts filled my mind, and you could physically feel the demonic presence. We all began to rebuke the enemy with the word, Bible scriptures. I began to declare the blood of Jesus against this foul manifestation. "The blood of Jesus is against you Satan and we have overcome you through it." The battle lasted about 5 to 8 minutes, and the demons broke and fled. We reached our destination and had a wonderful meeting with a precious presence of the Holy Spirit. There were salvations, healing, many touched and refreshed by the Spirit, and what I remember the most is a young couple came who were separated, and God healed their marriage. My traveling companion received a Word of Knowledge about their situation, and the problem was resolved. One word from God can destroy the enemy's plans of destruction.

There were many trips on trains where we would rent a sleeper cabin traveling from Bucharest, Romania to Sophia, Bulgaria where fighting principalities and powers was commonplace. One close couple who were prayer warriors for me had related a picture vision God had given one of them. They saw warring angels in the heavens above us and ministering spirits on the ground working hand in hand with us.

Hebrews 1:14 "Are they not all ministering spirits sent forth to minister for them who shall be heirs of salvation."

In short, we had air cover, and some unseen special agents, who I was told were huge, with awesome swords. God's kingdom is a kingdom of power. Team ministry, with every gift supplied and God getting all the glory, is where light invades the darkness and souls are liberated! Man's agenda must be put on the altar with his self-seeking ambitions. We need to know God's purposes and strategy.

God pours out his power on his tactics for his battle plan. When our flesh gets involved, it won't be long till manipulation starts. God doesn't bless our mess.

THE "BEAR" NECESSITY

The last example I'll use happened during a backpacking trip in the Bitterroot Mountains in southwestern Montana. On our first expedition there we hiked to the Nine-Mile Meadow where we were to camp that night and go deeper into the wilderness the following morning. An unforeseen storm rolled in and just sat over us. That night a bear visited our camp and a young man with us had his head bounced, right through the side of the tent. The three of us were like drowned rats, so we packed up and booked out of there. Cold and wet is bad enough but put a bear in the area and I'm all in for a hot shower, meal and bed! Bye, bye!

Now that little experience was the setup for this testimony. I think it was about a year and a half later I was back in the area again. The colleague I traveled with internationally resided there. This next trip we had four adults and two young teens. It was a 10-day trip up beyond the tree line to Blodgett Lake, about a 15- or 16-mile hike from the trailhead. We camped in the trail the first night. A rather nasty non-social dog was part of our company. He was to warn us if any unwanted animals were in or around camp. That night that mutt barked and went crazy all night. There was some terrific crashing and breaking going on in the woods. Some commotion for sure – and no sleep!

In the morning, we packed up, had a dry breakfast, and proceeded to hike up what felt like a 75-degree grade all day. And if that wasn't stressful enough, that unruly mutt of a dog was dead set on sinking his fangs into Kevin. This was beginning to turn into Pilgrim's Progress, second edition!

We reached the high meadow next to the lake and what a grand, beautiful view we beheld. We fished, fellowshipped, and of course scoured the landscape on a never-ending quest to find firewood. I was always concerned about my friend's slack approach to food management. He never would police the area or use my airtight bag to hoist our food up into a tree outside camp. This neglect was the setup for the testimony I will highlight.

It was about 6 days into the trip when the camp had settled down, everyone had gone to sleeping bags. The three younger men were sleeping next to the fire, each trying to display their own masculinity. My tent was set up on the wooded side of camp next to a boulder and small trees and brush. I like to take advantage of natural windbreaks when possible. My other cohorts set up lakeside out in the open, adjacent to me. I'd gotten all zipped into my down sleeping bag. Ya' know, cool mountain air is great for sleeping if you can stay on your rollout pad and dodge any missed rocks beneath you. I was sound asleep in no time.

My guess it was about 2:00 or 2:30 a.m. when I abruptly awoke. The first thing I did was listen for that dumb dog, but all was quiet. The bear conversation in camp was always on and off and we were all laughing about the joke of the missing hiker. They couldn't find him but found scat that smelled like pepper spray and had bear bells in it.

As I'm reflecting on that stupid joke, I hear that still, small voice tell me to get my boots on and go out and stoke the fire up, there's an animal coming up the trail. This trail led to the spring where we had been getting our water. Right away, I dismissed this as my own conscience playing with me.

Finally the Holy Spirit got my attention when the voice wasn't still or quiet when he said, "Put your boots on now, take your 9mm and both extra clips and get out now and stoke the fire." Remember, there are three people in sleeping bags laying out under the stars.

My fast thinking tells me a 9mm pistol and a bear make for a bad end to me! I quickly obeyed the firm directive and hauled my freight to the fire and got that puppy going about five feet high. It's like Christmas eve out there, nothing's stirring, all are asleep, and that no good dog – nothing!

So, I'm thinking and praying, "God, what in the world's going on?" I was careful not to stare into the fire to blind my sight. I'm starting to sweat now, can't tell if it's the warmth of the fire or the predicament.

All of a sudden, I can hear heavy movement in the brush and leaves rattling behind my tent! I don't care how spiritual you are, this was an "Oh no!" moment.

Now the muscle in my left thigh is jumping up and down and the adrenaline is in full flow. I chambered a round in my semi-automatic 9mm, ready for what may come! The best chance for these boys on the ground was clear: a 30-yard run for the lake.

Just then the Lord spoke to me, clear as a bell, and said the following: "This is what it's like protecting my sheep." Well, I guess that's what I was doing. I'm living a profound message from my Father in heaven. For some reason, the animal just moved away from the camp. It had to be hard because we had eaten Indian fry bread, like doughnuts, that day. I'm sure their aroma was still around.

I stayed awake till the sun hit the peaks, just in case, and so the fire was roaring. Still a bit bewildered I trudged off to my tent, put my sidearm on safety, kicked off my boots, zipped back in my bag, and started reflecting on this episode. I asked, "Father, it didn't come into the camp. How come?" His answer to me, "It couldn't cross the bloodline you've been praying around the camp since that first night on the trail." It was an overwhelming moment, to say the least.

Thank God for the blood of Jesus that, by faith, we can have protection from what the enemy can bring against us through praying the bloodline.

WHAT DOES THE BIBLE SAY ON THIS MATTER?

There is no clear cut passage, but there is a precedent. A bloodline started just outside the Garden of Eden with the blood from animals and furs to cover Adam and Eve, Passover at Exodus, to the scarlet cord that hung out of Rahab the harlot's window. All symbolized Christ's blood. Think of King David while bringing back the Ark of the Covenant to Jerusalem in 2 Samuel 6:12, 13. Every six paces he sacrificed oxen and fatted sheep. Animal blood on the doorposts in Egypt is nothing in comparison to Jesus' holy, pure atonement for us. When you are saved, you're trusting by faith his blood is sufficient to cleanse all your sins and make them white as snow.

We again need to honor and value Jesus' blood. When I was first saved we sang about the blood. We thanked God and reverenced its power. So using faith to trust the blood of Jesus for a line of protection is not out of order. Humility and thanksgiving will fortify our confidence. We speak things that aren't as though they are (2 Corinthians 4:18) while we do not look at the things which are seen, but at the things which are not seen.

Another verse that applies to this is 2 Corinthians 4:13, 14. And since we have the same spirit of faith, according to what is written, "I believed and therefore I spoke." We also believe and therefore speak! Knowing that he who raised up the Lord Jesus will also raise us up with Jesus, and will present us with you.

Faith is expressed by words spoken from a heart that is persuaded by the truth of spiritual reality, that is, not seen by our physical senses. Seeing, feeling, hearing, touch, taste, or smell don't reveal supernatural kingdoms that surround us. They show us the aftermath of good or evil. This is why it's imperative that Biblical signs and wonders accompany the declaration of God's Kingdom and his Gospel!

Mark 16:20 "And they went out and preached everywhere, the Lord working with them and confirming the Word with signs following."

When the kingdom of God's Gospel is preached, there is always results. We again need the finger of God to be revealed in our meetings.

Luke 11:20 Jesus speaking here: "But if I cast out demons with the finger of God, surely the kingdom of God has come upon you."

Whip the enemy!

I think it's important to pray the bloodline over your children, travel, business, home, and relationships. Add this to your defensive armor in Ephesians 6, as well as the sword of the Spirit and the name of

Jesus. I'm trying to put some fight back in you! Most all things coming against you can be defeated. Confess the blood, declare it, sing about it, and use it in the face of your enemy.

Win in this life, you have already won in the life to come!

You will never receive
your inheritance
by begging for
what is legally yours.
Receive it by simple faith
as you did salvation, through faith
in the Grace of God. It's impossible
to please God without believing
He is a rewarder of those
that search out, investigate, crave,
demand, and diligently worship Him.
(Hebrews 11:6; #1567)

CHAPTER 24

Healing Through The Blood

Jesus is the door to the sheepfold of God (John 10:7).

We covered Jesus' flesh being the veil of the temple in Heaven. When we believe on Christ with simple faith, we are passing through his punishment, sustained in his body for our sin. So, spiritually speaking, we approach God through our atoner's flesh.

I was always taught that Jesus suffered 39 stripes, save one. The truth is a cat-of-nine-tails swung against Jesus delivered 351 lashes, tearing his flesh. His whole torso was pulverized. Muscle, tendons, nerves, and bone were exposed. Jesus had to fulfill all prophecy spoken about him in the Old Testament. He was brought as a lamb to the slaughter.

Isaiah 53:1-7 "The Lord laid on him the iniquity of us all."

Isaiah 53:4-5 "Surely he hath borne our griefs, and carried our sorrows, yet we did esteem him stricken, smitten of God, and afflicted. But he was wounded for our transgressions, he was bruised for our iniquities, the chastisement of our peace was laid upon him, and with his stripes we are healed."

In verse 4, I want to look at the original text and definition of two words to obtain the truth. The words are "grief" and "sorrows," nouns. Grief is the Hebrew word kholee: malady, anxiety, calamity, disease. Grief is sickness, weakness, affliction. We see both physical healing and emotional healing. How can one receive physical healing when their emotional realm isn't sound enough to understand forgiveness and the love behind grace. This again is the reason we must renew our mind and rightly interpret the Bible through the death, burial, and resurrection of Christ. Not traditional religious thinking.

The Hebrew word for sorrows is makob: pain, sorry, affliction of grief. Both nouns Jesus bore or carried to his cross and are a part of our redemption. Atonement for complete healing flowed from the stripes leveled against Jesus for our transgressions, and twisted character distorted by our sin nature.

Paid in full is the total redemption from the fall of Adam. Sozo is the Greek word for save and noun soteria for salvation.

Romans 1:16 "For I am not ashamed of the Gospel of Christ, for it is the power of God unto salvation to everyone that believeth."

The Hebrew definition of salvation (4991) is: rescue or safety, deliver, health, salvation. (5020) deliver, protect, heal, preserve, save, do well, be or make whole. Wholeness, nothing broken and nothing missing in your life.

For God to put sickness on one of his children, he must deny the payment and sacrifice he had Jesus yield to in the Garden of Gethsemane. It's not even a rational debate. Or to nullify part of our redemption by teaching God does not recognize what Jesus did for our wholeness. We get into problems not taking responsibility for our temple or giving place to the devil.

1 Cor 10:13 "There's no temptation that is uncommon to man, but God is faithful who will not permit you to be tempted above that you are able; but will with the temptation also make a way to escape, that you may be able to bear it."

Jesus in the wilderness found out how to win. He used the Word and then was strengthened by angels. He's our example.

Ephesians 4:26-27 "Be ye angry, and sin not; let not the sun go down on your wrath; neither give place to the devil."

"Place," topos in the Greek, means opportunity or room (in your life). A foothold can turn into a beachhead attack to destroy you. Oppression is the result. In this world we will have trouble and some tribulations, but we're to be cheerful folks because the way maker has overcome. When times are restful, that's a good time to be in preparation, learning, renewing our minds to think and respond with Kingdom principles.

As you renew your mind and meditate on the Word of God, truth will move from head knowledge to revelation knowledge, transforming your mind, will, and emotions. Then when you speak, the Holy Spirit in you will empower your words as long as your motivation is pure and are moved by love. They become rhema anointed containers infused with power by the Holy Spirit.

Blood flowed from every stripe Jesus received for us to bring about the cure for humanity's need.

II Corinthians 1:20 "For the promises of God in Him are yes, and in Him amen, to the glory of God through us."

So if the promises are yes to you and yours in Christ, it boils down to receiving what has already been given to you. You've got God's word on it and He always is watching over his word to perform it.

Numbers 23:19 "God is not a man, that He should lie, nor the son of man, that He should repent. Has He said and will He not do? Or has He spoken and shall He not make it good?"

It's pivotal that you see yourself in Christ.

Humble yourself into God's mercy.
Change your wineskin!

CHAPTER 25

A New Identification

Pride can be manifested in numerous ways. False humility is one of the most detrimental forms. It will raise its head by a mentality that says, "I'm not good enough for God to do that for me," etc. You are never ever going to be good enough. We all merit through our performance a hot eternity.

True humility agrees with what the Bible says about us as believers in Jesus Christ.

2nd Corinthians 5:21 tells us that God gives us his very own righteousness when we are in Jesus.

Romans 8:15 "We have received the spirit of adoption whereby we cry, 'Abba, Father!'" You're a family member!

2nd Corinthians 5:17 "Therefore, if any man be in Christ, he is a new creation. The old has gone, the new has come."

Ephesians 2:5-6 "We have been raised up together, and made us sit together in heavenly places in Christ Jesus."

Romans 5:17 "We shall reign in life by one, Jesus Christ." You can control your personal life and help change circumstances for others.

The list of scriptures are nearly endless, but the fact remains that until you realize who you are and take your position in Christ, you'll always be a carnal believer, magnifying self-pity in your failure to perform some perfect standard that your heavenly Father did not set. It will never be attainable. So your identification will be as a continuous sinner, saved by grace that your security is based on how well you keep repenting in your condemnation brought by the devil while you try to keep all the law. What a cycle of defeat! Doctrines of devils can yoke us in while Jesus' yoke is light and brings rest to your soul.

See yourself on the cross with Jesus. As you put yourself there, it will profoundly change your identification! You are who God says you are, not the devil or those whom he lies through!

Galatians 2:20 (KJV) "I am crucified with Christ; nevertheless, I live; yet not I, but Christ liveth in me: and the life which I now live in the flesh I live by the faith of the Son of God, who loved me, and gave himself for me."

He also took the cup after supper, saying, "This is the New Covenant in my blood which is shed for you."

CHAPTER 26

A Continuing Covenant Meal

We can see clearly that the Lord's last supper began as the Passover meal and ended in a blood covenant meal.

This covenant meal was conducted as a sign of the New Testament in Jesus' blood, which was shed for us. It has forever replaced the Passover feast for the born-again believer.

Luke 22:19-20 "And he took bread, and gave thanks, and brake it and gave unto them, saying, 'This is my body, which is given for you; this do in remembrance of me. Likewise also the cup after supper saying, 'This cup is the new testament in my blood, which is shed for you.'"

Jesus told his disciples to "do this in remembrance

of me" (Luke 4:19). The Apostle Paul sheds more light in 1 Corinthians 11:26.

"For as often as ye eat this bread and drink this cup, ye do proclaim the Lord's death till he comes."

We too, are proclaiming Christ's sacrifice for our eternal life. We hope in the same resurrection as our Lord. If Christ died in vain, let's eat, drink and be miserably merry for tomorrow we die.

Those who do not understand the significance of Jesus' body and blood, the purpose of his suffering and death, will err with a religious mindset, and not receive the benefits of salvation. Taking the elements of communion irreverently, having not decided mentally or spiritually the significance will bring harm against those who live by the law. Totally missing the full benefits that have been purchased for them. Some are sick and weak and dead when, in Christ they could be strong, alive, and healthy (1 Corinthians 11:28-32).

Cults that were derived from true Christianity are more dangerous than one can imagine.

However, the great significance of partaking in the Lord's supper is a revelation of our relationship with the Godhead and the blood covenant that reassures our hearts of Jesus' commitment to us, and our response to his love poured out on Calvary for us.

Luke 4:4 tells us man cannot live by bread alone, but by every word of God. God's words are containers of spiritual life that, when accepted and applied, release peace and joy. Proverbs has a passage that states, "Mark the perfect man . . . his end is peace." He lives with peace within not subject to exterior circumstance. Jesus' flesh represents the living Word of God that walked on earth amongst his creation. He replaced manna or provision to sustain life in the wilderness after the Exodus. Jesus gave his flesh as the bread to bring true life to the spirit of man. His flesh housed the blood he shed to establish the New Testament covenant.

The Lord's Supper is a vital practice to realign, adjust, be healed and strengthened in spirit, soul, and body. We should look on this practice with anticipation of how our Savior will manifest in the reverent celebration of his love.

Jesus said in Matthew 26:29, "I will not drink of

the fruit of the vine from now on until that day when I drink it new with you in my father's kingdom."

We will partake together with Christ, arrayed in white fine linen at the Marriage Supper of the Lamb described in Revelation 19. His bride will behold him in his resurrected glory in heaven, clothed with a vesture dipped in blood: and his name is called the Word of God.

Keep your eyes fixed on your High Priest. He's coming quickly.

Maranatha!

Don't fear what's defeated.
Be bold. "I've overcome the world,"
and, "Lo, I am with you
to the end of the age."

CHAPTER 27
Conclusion

God's love has provided all you need. His mercy has released grace through Christ that saves to the uttermost.

Jesus' blood atonement for you is working now!

It was provided for you before you were ever born, and while you were yet a sinner. You can't achieve through religious works what is freely offered.

You must choose between freedom and liberty through relationship, or bondage and performance to the law. The one leads to eternal life in Christ. The other to eternal life in hell. I see it as a no-brainer! Just stop trying to manipulate your Heavenly Father and give your life away. He will take you and heal your wounds, making you whole with a new purpose in life.

It's hard to be a religious hypocrite. With all the work of pretending and acting. Always trying to be better than others. Just quit it and embrace grace. Crucify your pride; it's keeping you in condemnation. If your aim is just being better than the other guy, he may be on his way to hell. Jesus is the perfect standard. How are you measuring up?

YOUR PASSOVER HAS RISEN
I have laid down my life that
You might find life,
And taken the sting of your
Death upon me.
So hide your life in my death
And raise up in me to everlasting life.
For through your faith my
Blood brings forgiveness, and
Acceptance in my beloved.
Yes, and I myself will keep
Your foot from falling, and present
You faultless before his glorious presence.
© 1997 Mark A. Lefler

Don't cast away your confidence in Jesus for self-righteousness. The Church Age is coming to an end. When you take part in the Lord's Supper, think of the direction given to the Jews in Exodus 12:11. Eat the Passover meal with your loins girded, your shoes on your feet, and your staff in your hand. The moments of our time on earth are ticking away. In the twinkling of an eye we're gone.

Bleach your garments in the blood of Jesus. It's the only agent that supernaturally removes the stains of sin.

His love for you is stronger than death.

*Jesus chose to suffer
in pain and torment
for you rather than
leave you in
Satan's dominion.*

www.ingramcontent.com/pod-product-compliance
Lightning Source LLC
LaVergne TN
LVHW052100090426
835512LV00036B/2852